Distributed in U.S. by:
Rizzoli International Publications, Inc.
597 Fifth Avenue
New York, New York 10017
Rizzoli ISBN 0-8478-5518-X

Distributed in Canada by:
Firefly Books
3520 Pharmacy Ave. Unit 1-C
Scarsborough, Ontario, Canada

Distributed in the United Kingdom by:
Internos Books
Colville Road
London, W3 8BL, England
Internos ISBN 0-904866-67-X

Distributed throughout rest of the world by:
Hearst Books International
105 Madison Avenue
New York, New York 10016

Published by:
American Showcase, Inc.
724 Fifth Avenue, 10th Floor
New York, New York 10019
(212) 245-0981
TLX: 880356 AMSHOW P

Design by: Henry Wolf
Printed and bound in Italy
by Amilcare Pizzi S p.A., Milan: First Printing
Typesetting by:
Characters Typographic Services
ISBN 0-931144-47-7
Library of Congress
Catalog Card No. 88-70889

Henry Wolf

Visual Thinking

methods
for making
images
memorable

American Showcase Inc.   New York

My portrait was taken
by a model after a long session,
who, after having had hundreds
of pictures taken of her,
wanted to take one of me.

A view of the studio
with its most important
fixture, the light,
which can be moved by
electric motors in any direction.
All the wires are overhead,
off the floor. In the box
is one electronic flash head
that gives off a constant
amount and color of light.
In ten years,
it only failed once.

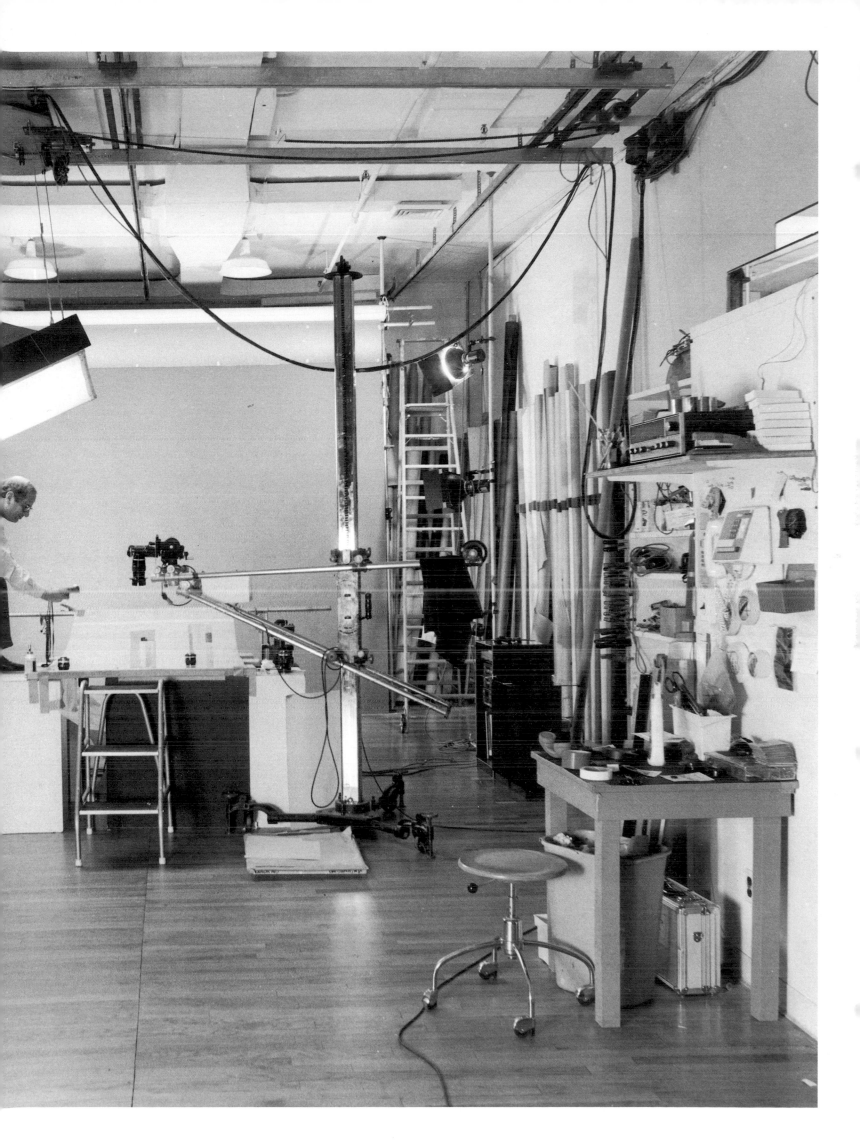

Contents

About This Book

I had many choices in organizing this book, and there probably was not one correct way. I could have shown my work in chronological order. Another solution would have been to separate editorial from advertising, or color from black and white, or people from still life. Instead, I chose a way which I hope will serve as something more than an anthology or, worse, an ego trip.

For many years in teaching design, I have taken the point of view that the creation of images is really an act of translation. You can translate English into French or you can translate English into "Picture." All design activity, all advertising, all films start with the word. We read a synopsis before doing a book jacket, a script before shooting a film, and research before doing a layout for an ad. An architect talks with his client before designing a house. From words describing the family's size, the architect learns how many bathrooms will be needed.

Certain techniques and certain tricks come into play when you transform words into imagery. This book represents an attempt at isolating some of these methods for making images more compelling, more unique and therefore more memorable. Many of the examples in these pages could have been repeated in different chapters, so I had to decide which trick had the starring role. For example, in "Unexpected Combinations," humor is also often present. The surrealists, who knew the value of surprise and shock, often ended up with humor as a by-product.

In a back-handed compliment, a photographer once said that he didn't know whether I was the best Art Director, but he was sure I was the fastest editor. What he was implying was that I didn't agonize enough over which of his pictures to pick, that I was quick and therefore careless. What he didn't know was that I fall in love with a photograph—my reaction is immediate. It is much easier to do that with someone else's work than with your own. Selecting from your own work is so much harder, because you know too much about its background. It could be that you arrived at a solution that now looks obvious only after long and frustrating experimentation. Conversely, the idea might have come in a flash, effortlessly. The history

attached to a piece of work does not have much to do with its graphic or photographic merit. I always found that I did my best work at my different jobs between the day I resigned and the day I actually left. There were those few weeks of wonderful freedom from fear and pressure.

My design activity has often ended up in results other than the printed page, but it is the magazine, the book, the thing you can hold in your hand at will, unchanging over time, that remains my favorite.

I can almost put an exact date on the beginning of this love affair. In the fall of 1938, when I was thirteen and living in a small pension in Versailles with my family (who were refugees from Nazi-occupied Austria), my father's bachelor uncle came to visit from London. He had brought with him the current issue of Esquire Magazine and forgot it in his room when he left. I found it and later carried it with me through France, Morocco and to New York. I loved the feel of the glossy paper, the smell of the printed pages, the girls, the serious writing. On bad days I opened that magazine and a promise of a wonderful sort of life emanated from its pages like a seductive perfume. Fifteen years later I started working for Esquire. Life sometimes plays wonderful tricks.

I hope this book hits the right balance between being instructive, nostalgic and, on two or three pages, inspirational.

9

Preface

Is it so important in this age of nuclear threat, AIDS, terrorism and polyester shirts that magazine covers, building entrances, corporate logos, lipstick ads or abstract collages be beautiful?

Was it important that Haydn played beautifully at Prince Esterházy's musical soirées for 80 people? That Dürer signed his etchings in much more elegant lettering than is available from all of today's computer typesetting marvels? That Stradivari treated the wood of the violins he built for a handful of clients in Cremona in a way that hasn't been duplicated in four centuries?

Yes. The answer is <u>yes</u>, it is important. It is the small monuments, the details that are the milestones of civilization; they accumulate to make history. Sometimes I feel that we are near the entrance to a tunnel leading into a long night, and we must leave marks before the darkness. This is not the first time that mankind has been at such an impasse: the armless Venuses of Greece and the murals of Pompeii have survived the long night that followed the golden age of Rome. And then the cathedrals started to rise; Gutenberg's movable type made it possible to disseminate ideas. Suddenly art was everywhere—in Florence and Venice and in Germany, in Holland, in Austria and Spain. Henry VIII remains with us because of Holbein's portrait, as do Vivaldi and Bach because of a few ink marks on some pieces of paper which, when piled up on the floor, would not even reach as high as a man's head.

Some works of art are by nature unrecordable. The cook at the Court of Louis XIV may have prepared culinary masterpieces of which we have no knowledge. Casanova's lovemaking may still be unsurpassable or it may simply be a legend, an early press agent's fabrication. Molière's actors could have been great or cornier than Rodney Dangerfield. It is the words, the plays themselves that survive undiminished. Certainly more people heard Mozart's music by watching the film "Amadeus" than during his lifetime and all the years thereafter.

With imagery there is a legacy. It was Jorge Luis Borges who said: "Painters after death become books—not a bad incarnation." We can look back at our few thousand years of his-

Albrecht Dürer's colophon.

1932 Packard taillight.

Henry VIII.

tory because they are made up of these landmarks. Paintings, buildings, sculptures, novels, photographs, sonatas, and, yes, dresses, door handles, posters and watch faces become guideposts in looking back. The taillight of a 1932 Packard evokes the USA in the thirties as much as a Fitzgerald novel does.

Enormous quantity and high quality have seldom gone hand in hand. There will be more imagery produced and reproduced in this one year than in all of history before World War II. Even though we now have infinitely more imagery, it is hardly better. Our mania for preserving, xeroxing, microfilming, videotaping hasn't raised our standards of excellence, and mediocrity may yet overwhelm us by its sheer volume. More than ever, more than in the times of Pericles, Rembrandt or Whistler, it is important to create worthwhile words, music and images. History will examine our era, and we must leave a decent report card.

Stradivari: Violin, 1691.

1 Unexpected Combinations

It may be possible to distinguish between two kinds of images.

The first kind represents something that exists in reality, and its form is recognizable in the final picture. The interpretation of this reality is always changed by the artist's vision, by a prevalent style, by fashion, by technique; but the original source remains evident through the transfiguration.

The second kind of image has never existed before as a whole entity. Its source is not traceable to one model, one event, one original. It is either complete fantasy or a combination of at least two "real" sources. The extreme in this category is total abstraction, with no discernible pictorial source except for other art or imagery.

What I am concerned with here is the combination of two or more images that have existed—separately—before, but are now combined to form a new entity with a new meaning, a visual intersection not foreseen by traveling the obvious route.

The pictorial manifestations of this method are often very closely related to the written word; their origins are cerebral as opposed to visceral and instinctive. There is also, I suspect, a form of envy at play here, a longing for the simpler, more emotional process. It is easier to "like" a Renoir nude than a Picabia machine collage done only a few decades later. Why then the need to intellectualize, to make a visual pun, to shock by strange associations rather than just create a beautiful rendition of seven apples and a napkin?

Perhaps the change came with all the other transformations precipitated by the Industrial Revolution. Until then, much of the picture maker's work was centered around religious beliefs, which provided a never-ending source of inspiration combined with almost endless financial resources. There was room for fantasy rendered realistically, because the subject matter itself was fantasy. After all, who has ever <u>seen</u> an angel?

Representational imagery became the province of the new patrons, the latter-day Medicis: the Industrialists. They needed realistic imagery

J.A.D. Ingres.
The Comtesse d'Haussonville, 1845.

Ingres' portrait
marks a high point in
representational art,
achieved shortly before
the advent of photography.
The perfect lady in
a perfect, real setting.

René Magritte.
The False Mirror, 1928.

The great surrealist
invents a scene that never
existed in reality
by combining two separate,
unrelated subjects.

Harry Callahan.
Eleanor, 1953.

Harry Callahan creates
a magical image with more
than one negative.
Photography, which started out
as the realistic, believable
medium, becomes fantasy by
juxtaposing several pictures.

for picturing the products of their manufactures. It is no accident that the photograph was invented at exactly that time of transition, becoming the ideal tool for making believable representations quickly and inexpensively. The inference was that since the object had to be in front of the camera to be photographed, the camera could not lie. The photograph thus became the believable image.

A new outlet for fantasy had to be found, and it was. Around the end of the century, the Impressionists and the Cubists started departing from realism. Monet's landscapes and Picasso's fractured portraits became masterpieces of this period of change. During and immediately after World War I, which finally marked the end of the old order in art and society, Surrealism and Dada came into full flower —and just as quickly faded. Their greater importance lies not so much in the works of a handful of artists, but in the lasting effect their techniques had on mass communication, advertising, illustration, and poster design. In spite of shortened cycles of obsolescence, their influence is still everywhere 60 years later. No other movement in art was ever so quickly adopted and adapted to a related but ideologically different discipline.

If there is one recurrent theme in the work of the Surrealists, it is the idea of unexpected combinations. When a subject is combined with another subject in an unorthodox way, the more surprising is the transformation and the more successful the statement. Surprise is also a key element of humor, as anyone who has ever analyzed the construction of a joke will understand. Humor is therefore a by-product of this technique and often present in its manifestations.

Another result of juxtaposing elements that do not belong together is shock, a reaction the Dadaists were very fond of. The cutting of an eyeball with a straight razor in Dali's film The Andalusian Dog, Duchamp's urinal as sculpture, or Meret Oppenheim's furlined teacup are examples of this need to shock the viewer.

The working method that accomplishes these results is not easy to quantify. There are two major categories: addition—in which one or more elements are added to an image; and substitution—in which part of an image is replaced by another that does not normally belong with it. The visual examples that follow demonstrate this process.

Luis Buñuel. Un chien andalou, 1924.

Meret Oppenheim.
Object, 1936.

A cover for
American Photographer
Magazine featuring
a story on my work.
I combined my
self-portrait with
my favorite subject.

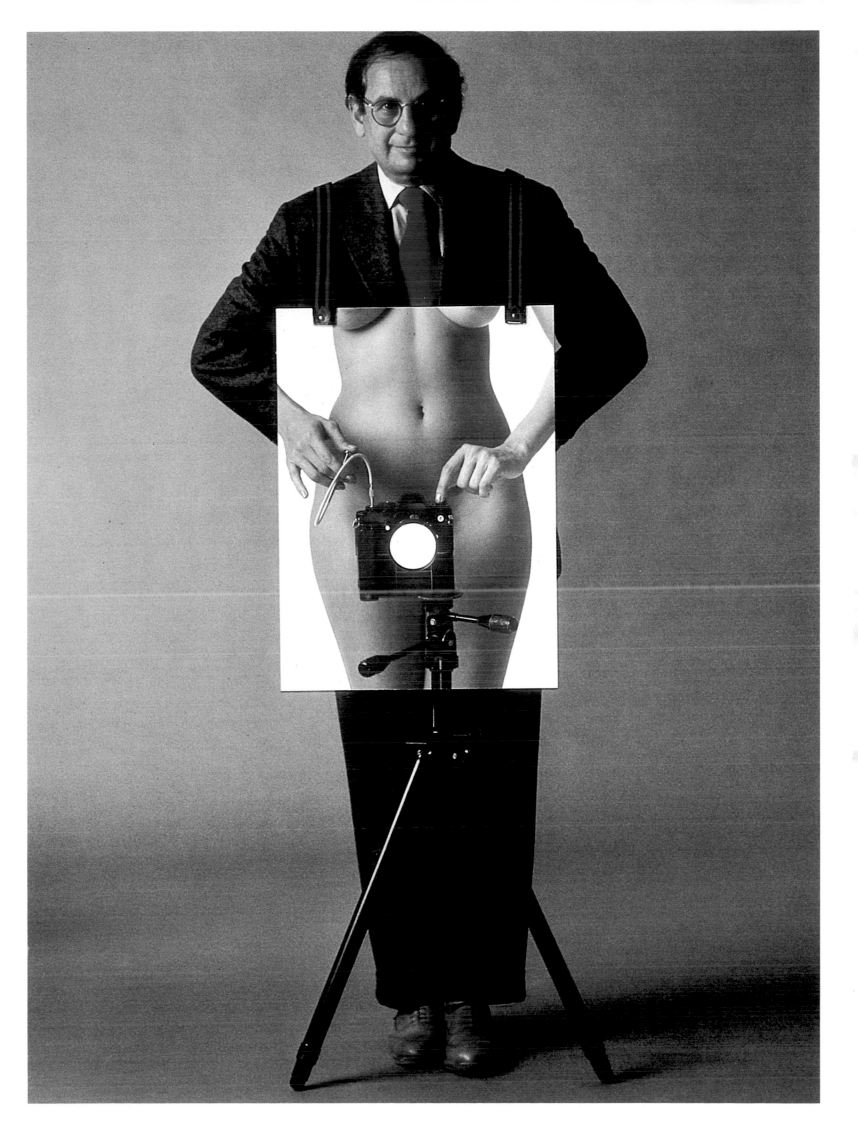

An illustration for
Money Magazine.
The theme was
the business lunch.
I combined the participants
and the prop in an
unexpected way, taking
the two martini lunch
one step further:
they are having lunch
in the glass.

This was the last cover of
Esquire I was responsible
for (over 70 others had
preceded it).
The lead article was about
the Americanization of Paris,
so I combined France's
passion for red wine
with the U.S.A.'s predilection
for fast (or "instant") food.
Esquire got hundreds
of letters asking where
this fictitious product
could be purchased.

JULY, 1958
PRICE 60¢

Esquire

MAGAZINE FOR MEN

INSTANT VIN ROUGE

FORD FRICK:
RELUCTANT CZAR

THE FOUR LIVES
OF WM. BENTON

THE COMPLEAT
SECRETARY

THE AMERICANIZATION OF PARIS

Two illustrations for a book
about Xerox Corporation
produced by
Chermayeff and Geismar.
Both are concerned with
areas where Xerox is active.
One pictures Wall Street
in better days, and
the other highlights a
new opaque paper used
in x-ray photos that
was one of Xerox's many
contributions to
the field of medicine.

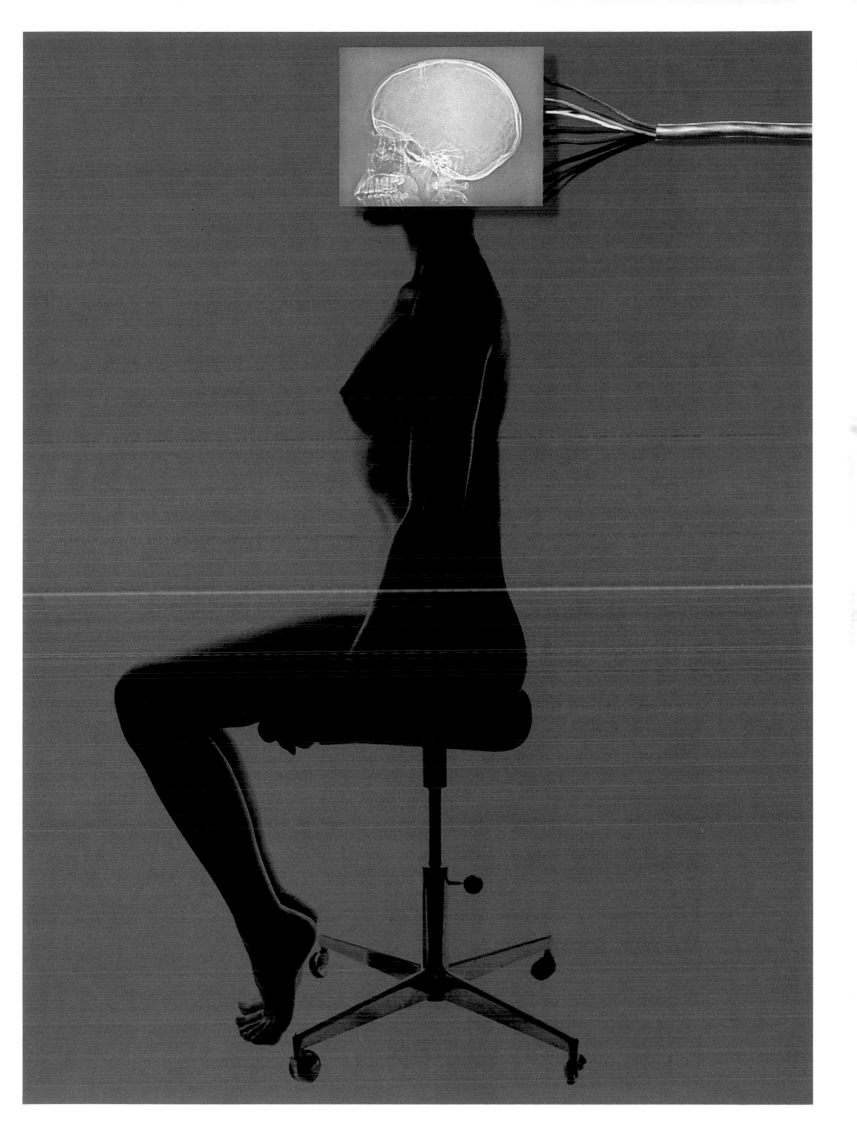

A cover for a
wine issue of
New York Magazine
where the model
actually wore
14 pounds of grapes.
Milton Glaser
was the Art Director.

A cover of
Holiday Magazine.
Frank Zachary,
the editor,
said,"The story should be
about 'Tunisia being
a state of mind'."

A public service ad
for Ogden Industries
done in the late '60s.
The headline was
"Next?"
and the idea was
not to discriminate
against young people
with long hair—
Einstein's hairstyle
resembled the hippies',
and one of them might
turn out to be
the next great genius.

A <u>Bazaar</u> cover.
Partially obscuring
the type with
the gloves results in
a three-dimensional effect.

An ad for a Revlon product
that claims to
slow down the effects
of time on skin.

A one-eyed driver has a hard time judging the distance between himself and an oncoming car.

In "normal" perspective rendering, the horizon is 5½ feet up. The convention is that vertical lines stay vertical, while horizontals converge to a vanishing point on a horizon which is level with the viewer's eyes. All that changes in a worm's eye view of a room or when looking down at St. Peter's Dome. Artists have often attempted to break away from these rules of normal perspective. In an analysis of one of the painter de Chirico's masterpieces, there is evidence that he has used five or more vanishing points.

Oriental art employs a different convention to create the illusion of depth. Objects or scenes are simply placed one behind the other. The ones closer to the viewer overlap the more distant ones. Typically, a cherry tree in the foreground covers part of Mt. Fuji.

Still another method is to create distortions different from any your eyes have ever seen. In photography, a lens with a focal length of around 50mm on a 35mm camera creates an image very similar to what a normal viewer might see. A 20mm lens creates an image no human eye has ever seen. Things are very far apart, the foreground is bigger, the background small. Conversely, a 400mm lens compresses perspective, and the opposite is true. Who hasn't seen pictures where a red setting sun is four times the size of the sailboat in the foreground?

One of Cubism's many innovations was to depict a person or an object from different points of observation simultaneously. The painter walked around the subject and superimposed two or more views. Einstein (at about the same time as Picasso) used the idea of simultaneous observation from different vantage points for his theoretical illustrations in *The Theory of Relativity*, published in 1905.

It is not my intention to get technical here, for there is neither room in these pages nor enough knowledge on my part to do so. The important point to remember is that a subject viewed from an unusual angle, or distorted in relation to normal vision, becomes interesting and commands attention.

Giorgio de Chirico. <u>Gare Montparnasse (The Melancholy of Departure)</u>, 1914.

The painter breaks with conventional perspective in this lonely, imaginary scene in which he uses many conflicting vanishing points.

The Nymph of the Lo River. Chinese scroll.

In Oriental art, distance is achieved by placement. The trees in the background are taller than the ones in the foreground and yet are clearly behind the figures.

A shark washed ashore photographed with an extreme wide-angle lens which creates the illusion of great distance.

An ad for Elizabeth Arden cologne. My problem was to avoid showing the model's footprints in the sand. By having her walk in a straight line from the horizon, I was able to cover them by her body in the shot.

Six members of the modern dance group Pilobolus shown in an unusual view.

An ad campaign for Herman Miller dramatizing the problems that can occur when you buy office furniture without planning. The desk used as a prop was 100 feet wide.

Malcolm Forbes' eyeglasses.

A poster for a series of lectures
at the Rochester Institute of Technology.
My view of "The Impact of Excellence"
is that you walk above the crowd.

A poster for an IBM television
special on Shakespeare.
Actor Ian McKellen enters
the stage with Shakespeare's
portrait as a backdrop.

Ian McKellen
Acting Shakespeare

A brilliant actor's
celebration
of the world's
greatest
playwright

Saturday, January 15 on PBS
8PM*

*PLEASE CHECK YOUR LOCAL TV LISTINGS

IBM

The Impact of Excellence

A symposium
in celebration
of 150 years of
photography
and design:

Peter Bunnell
Cornell Capa
Dr. Harold Edgerton
Morton Goldsholl
Allen Hurlburt
Nathan Lyons
Sidney Rapoport
Pete Turner
Henry Wolf

May 14 & 15
Rochester
Institute
of
Technology

George H. Clark
Memorial
Gymnasium
Rochester, N.Y.

Sponsored by Rochester Institute of
Technology and Eastman Kodak
Company in cooperation with
Professional Photographers of America, Inc.

3 Repetition

An ad for the department store
Bergdorf Goodman.
The image on the
ground glass is an
upside down duplicate
of the model.

When I was a child, we would sometimes get a
tin box of cookies on which there was an elaborate printed label. It showed an exotic looking
lady holding the same box of cookies, on which
there was a label of a lady holding the same
box, and so on ad infinitum. This device is an
age-old one, but still effective. The viewer is
compelled to try and count how many stages of
repetition he can discern before the image is
reduced to illegibility. This is only one example
of repetition as visual seduction. It is effective
for the same reason as most of the other methods in this book: the image is one removed from
normal human vision.

Another device quite different in effect is the
kaleidoscope. Instead of the picture becoming
smaller and smaller, it is repeated in sections,
side by side, all the same size. The most banal
objects become interesting when they are
refracted and repeated in eight identical fragments by means of a system of prisms.

The mirror has always fascinated artists. It is
the only device by which we can see ourselves,
and yet not quite—because left and right are
interchanged, which is no small change. The
only car accident I've ever had in 40 years of
driving was in England, because I could not get
used to driving on the left side of the road. I
once took a head-on shot of a well-known photography model, made two reversed prints,
then made a face out of the two left sides of the
face and another of the two right sides. The two
resulting photographs did not look like a portrait of the same person.

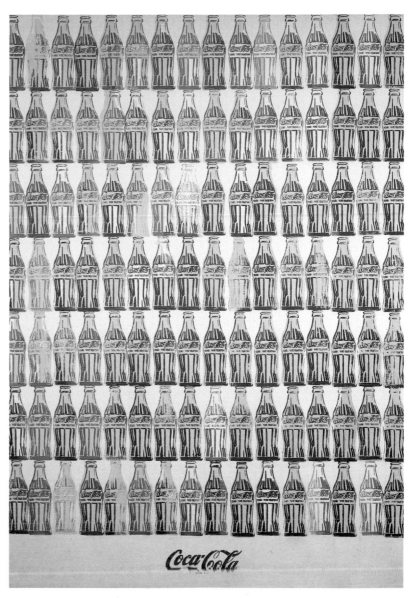

Andy Warhol. Green Coca-Cola Bottles, 1962.

Warhol's art poked fun
at the insistent repetition
in advertising's promotion
of world-class products.

Repetition is the darling of advertising. A message spoken only once is a whisper in the woods, while a message repeated a thousand times is inescapable, often annoying but always remembered. Advertisers such as Coca-Cola with centi-million dollar yearly budgets don't need to be too creative in their ads or their TV commercials. The imprint is subliminal just by being endlessly repeated. Conversely, a small boutique in Soho has to get attention by being original and artful; its budget does not allow for effectiveness by repetition. Years ago, there were two beautiful twin girls in New York who worked as photography models. They were almost always booked as a pair. The fascination was not with their beauty, but that there were two of them who looked almost alike.

In a way, repetition is the opposite of surprise, the reverse of shock. At its most extreme, it is close to Chinese water torture. At its best, it is appreciated because most people don't like to be surprised.

The Marx Brothers' classic
A Night at the Opera
was one of many comedies
repeating expected
comic situations.

Recently in Paris, I saw people standing in a long line to see a movie. At first I thought it was a new hit, but soon found out it was the old Marx Brothers classic,   A Day at the Races. Fifty years after the making—in another country, in a strange language—the public still loves their films because the action is always as expected. Chico plays the piano with one finger, Harpo toots his horn, and Groucho chases rich ladies a foot taller than he is. Repetition worked for them for decades.

33

This <u>Photographis</u> cover
shows a nude imagining
herself dressed as
she peers in the mirror.

A portrait of the French actress
Aurore Clément, famous for
her role as a Nazi collaborator
in Louis Malle's film,
<u>Lacombe, Lucien</u>.

THE BOLD LOOK
OF **KOHLER**

The first bath luxurious for one, spacious for two. No spout, making bathing much more pleasant and safe. The Infinity∞Bath™ Whirlpool has central controls, easy to reach from either end. In 17 fantastic colors and five or six foot lengths. For more details see the Yellow Pages, or send $2 to Kohler Co., Dept. AP3, Kohler, Wisconsin 53044.

© 1986 Copyright 1985 Kohler Co.

An ad from a campaign for Kohler bath fixtures. Endless repetition of an image creates depth.

An ad for Revlon on four different color make-up schemes, showing a kaleidoscopic view of the same face.

THE QUARTO COLOURINGS

A <u>Bazaar</u> cover for a special issue on water.

HARPER'S

BAZAAR

THE
WONDERS
OF WATER

EARLY
MEMOIRS
OF
SIMONE
DE
BEAUVOIR

INSIDER's
NEW YORK

MAY 1959
60 CENTS

For <u>Show</u> Magazine's feature
on summer reading,
we buried the model under
the sand in a coffin. A hole
had been drilled so that
her hand could emerge,
like a snail, from the earth.

A bellboy at the
Paris Ritz,
standing at attention
in the elevator of
the great hotel.

SHOW

THE MAGAZINE OF THE ARTS

75 CENTS
AUGUST 1962

MIDSUMMER SPECIAL:
Lolita's Private Life | Maugham's Memoirs | Lehar's Vienna | Ian Fleming's Workbook

4
Motion

In the 1950's, when I was art director of Esquire, I decided to give myself a photography assignment. The subject was a favorite of mine because it involved automobiles, and I thought I could do the job plus get a free trip. The assignment was to get pictures of a Grand Prix automobile race, so I bought myself the then most advanced 35mm camera, with an advertised shutter speed of 1/1000th of a second. Armed with a press pass and lots of film, I snapped away as the Ferraris, the Maseratis and the Jaguars were whipping by at 150 miles an hour, using my fast shutter speed for each shot. A week later in New York, I was very disappointed; I had hundreds of slides of parked cars. Luckily, in my nervousness, at one point I had inadvertently moved the shutter speed button to 1/60th of a second, and I had quite a wonderful shot of a red Ferrari streaking by the grandstand.

I had learned an important lesson. In still photography, motion has to be simulated and interpreted. Other photographers, notably the great Ernst Haas, had explored this for years, and painters like Duchamp and Balla had interpreted motion in their paintings decades earlier. But as in many other instances in my career, I had had to reinvent the wheel. The term "still photography" aptly describes one of the limits of this form of picture-making. As with the third dimension, motion is inherently missing so you have to create it, to inject it artificially.

Speed lines in comic strips are one of the simplest tricks for indicating motion. In photography, several methods can be used. You can follow the moving subject in your viewfinder and, while keeping pace with it, trip the shutter. The background will thus streak, and the subject—because it is not "moving" in relation to the camera—will be sharp. The opposite method is to keep your camera steady and let the subject streak by. The speed of the exposure depends on many factors: the distance from the subject, its speed, the focal length of the lens, and so on.

Multiple exposure is another way to simulate motion. The invention of the stroboscopic light has made it possible to get dozens of overlapping exposures of a golfer's swing. Now, we can not only stop a speeding bullet in mid-flight,

Marcel Duchamp.
Nude Descending a Staircase #2, 1912.

Duchamp in his famous,
controversial painting simulates
motion by overlapping
several stages of the action.
Forty years later Elisofon duplicates
the painting in photography
by using the artist as the model
in Life Magazine.

but we can combine many "still" shots of an
action onto a single negative. Eadweard Muybridge, in his famous 19th-century motion
studies, had to be content to take consecutive
photographs of a girl jumping a barrier, and
then place them side-by-side like a film strip.
In Duchamp's Nude descending a staircase,
the exact same technique of overlapping was
used, causing such a sensation that the painting was withdrawn from the Salon of 1912.

Eadweard Muybridge.
Animal Locomotion, 1887.

Electronic flash (more commonly called strobe)
gives off an extremely short burst of light, mea-
sured in hundredths or even thousandths of a
second. This gives photographers the chance
to freeze motion, and also to combine this
"freezing" with one of the other techniques
described. You can, for example, "streak"
a racing car with a slow shutter speed and, in
the middle of the exposure, also freeze it with
strobe, combining a sharp image of the car with
the illusion of speed.

A tiger from an
old circus poster jumps
from a die-cut cage
in a brochure
for Champion paper.

An illustration for a story
on dieting in <u>House Beautiful</u>.
Motion was achieved by
using a strobe plus
incandescent light,
a long exposure,
and by moving the camera.

A frontispiece for a
Christmas issue of
<u>Harper's Bazaar</u>.
When the shutter is
left open, the stars
trace lines on the film.

It is significant that it was the Wise Men
who followed the Star. It is
significant that the Star was nothing
in itself; its importance
lay in what it guided to: the Child.
That is to say, of course,
the infant Jesus; that is to say,
too, any child as such,
infinitely innocent and perfectible.
The gift of comprehension,
that gives us access
to the physical universe, also
makes us the inheritors of this explosive
concept of God-in-man. It is
the grain of mustard seed, more powerful
than any rocket, from which man's
spirit grows and flourishes
until it outdistances the stars.
This year when we gather
with our children at the tree
under the Christmas Star, and later,
perhaps, when we go out with them
to look at the night sky,
let us help them to see themselves
and all of starry space
with a sense of wonder,
and an awareness of sanctity,
in the light of the mysterious Star.

The hand of a cocaine dealer shot for an <u>Esquire</u> profile. The rings intensify the hitting power of his hand.

Illustration for an article on the great pianist Arthur Rubinstein. The lyrical bird flying from the piano is meant to symbolize his free and exuberant style.

LAWRENCE OF ARABIA

A book on the film <u>Lawrence of Arabia</u>; a slow shutter speed created the blur.

An illustration of motion for the IBM house organ, <u>Think</u>. Thin ribbons attached to a fan create the image.

If you came across a bottle labeled with a skull and crossbones, you would not be tempted to taste its contents. A red traffic light automatically makes your foot push the brake pedal. Symbols are graphic devices prompting you to action: sometimes warning of impending danger, other times informing or classifying. They are shorthand for complex ideas. Symbols overcome language barriers and provide instant recognition. The yellow box says Kodak, even if you are illiterate. The curly script says Coca-Cola, even before you read the words. Flags are symbols: the Union Jack means England, the red disc, Japan, the Stars and Stripes, America, reaffirming not just the fact but a lot of the legends around the fact. The symbol is a powerful conjurer of a thousand images, all at once. The danger in using symbols is the danger of the cliché: an effective symbol has always been seen a thousand times before. Milton Glaser's ingenious I ♥ New York has now been copied in hundreds of versions, varying from imitation to insanity.

Because of its ability to compel people to action, the symbol has become a selling tool. Companies are protecting their logotypes with copyrights and restricting their use via complicated manuals. Books governing the applications of the IBM or AT&T logos are the size of a small telephone directory. Updating or changing a trademark like Mobil's, replacing the prancing Pegasus with the updated red "O", cost close to a hundred million dollars.

For a designer or photographer, the use of the symbol depends on the ingenuity with which you apply it in a way different from its original intent. The surrealists picked on the Mona Lisa as "The Painting," not because it was the greatest painting ever made, but because of its fame, its history of having been stolen and returned. It was a perfect target. They defaced it, collaged it, paraphrased it, copied it, and each time it became even more "valuable." The Greek Pygmalion legend of the sculptor who shaped the perfect woman and made her come to life became G. B. Shaw's <u>Pygmalion</u> and later, in its third reincarnation, Lerner & Loewe's <u>My Fair Lady</u>. The symbol thrives on revival and is strengthened through each adaptation. It reduces misunderstandings created by language and other differences. Symbols are a reaffirmation of our basic sameness.

5
Manipulated Symbols

Jasper Johns. <u>Three Flags</u>, 1958.

The symbol, in repetition,
becomes more than the sum
of its parts.

In Milton Glaser's ingenious substitution
of a picture for a word,
the "heart" image actually reads as "love."

The Pygmalion legend in three incarnations:
As a 19th century painting; as the subject
of a film of G.B. Shaw's <u>Pygmalion</u>,
starring Leslie Howard and Wendy Hiller; and
as Lerner and Loewe's musical <u>My Fair Lady</u>,
starring Audrey Hepburn and Rex Harrison.

The assignment from <u>Audience</u> Magazine was to portray your personal view of Valentine's Day. Milton Glaser was the Art Director.

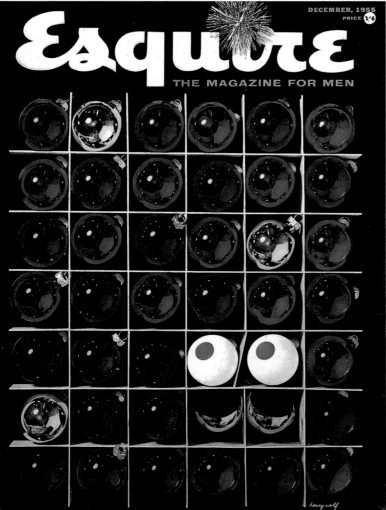

Two <u>Esquire</u> covers. The ogling playboy was <u>Esquire</u>'s symbol for nearly 30 years, and it was a game for readers to find him in yet another incarnation each month.

SHOW

INCORPORATING USA·I

THE
MAGAZINE
OF
THE
ARTS
75 CENTS
FEBRUARY 1963

SPACE RACE:
TOWARD
A RENAISSANCE?

MOTHER
TATTLES ON
TENNESSEE

"MAY WE BORROW
YOUR HUSBAND?"
A SHOCKING
NEW STORY
BY GRAHAM GREENE

OPERA VALENTINE: ANNA MOFFO

A slightly more sedate view
of Valentine's Day—
the heart as x-ray.
The model was the famous
opera singer Anna Moffo.

A broken heart is
stapled together in
this cover for a
book of love poems.

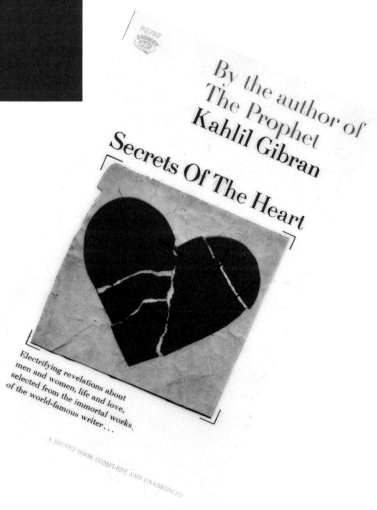

By the author of
The Prophet
Kahlil Gibran

Secrets Of The Heart

Electrifying revelations about
men and women, life and love,
selected from the immortal works
of the world-famous writer...

A SIGNET BOOK COMPLETE AND UNABRIDGED

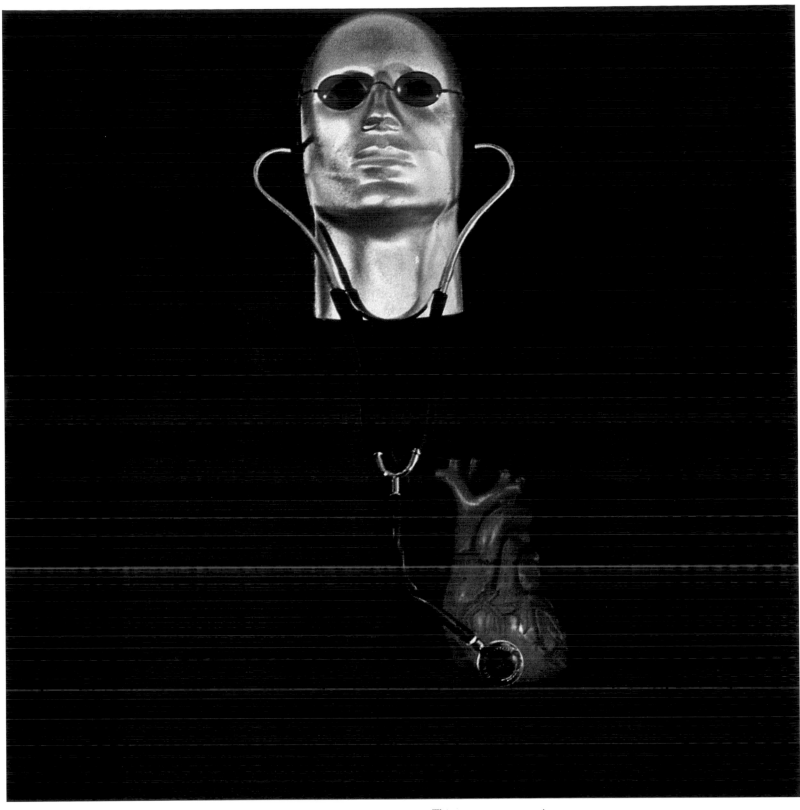

This strange construction
was one of 50 original works
done by 50 designers
to celebrate the
American Institute of Graphic Arts'
50th anniversary.
A small lightbulb inside
the plastic heart flashed
red intermittently by means
of an automatic switch.

A cookbook cover where
the French flag is an assemblage
of knife, fork and spoon.

WILLIAM AND CHESBROUGH RAYNER

T2685

FRENCH
COOKING
BY THE
CLOCK

A SIGNET BOOK

The lead story in this
1963 issue of Show was about
the Kennedy family, whose
portraits made up the flag.
The President asked for a framed copy.

SHOW

THE
MAGAZINE
OF
THE
ARTS

75 CENTS
APRIL 1963

INCORPORATING USA • 1

TOO MANY KENNEDYS? by ALISTAIR COOKE

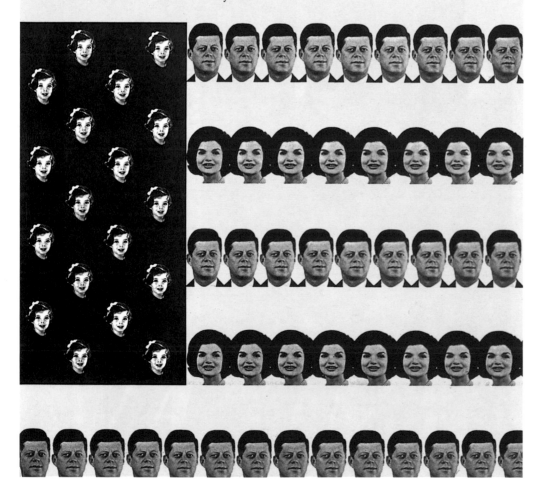

A poster for a Fourth of July
department store promotion
called "Wave It."
The Statue of Liberty
gets with it.

6
Scale

A subject can have scale only in relation to another subject. An elephant photographed against a white background has no scale, so a child who has never seen one would have no idea of its actual size. Place a man next to the elephant and the child would become aware of its hugeness.

I have never seen the Pyramids of Egypt, but I had a friend who made the trip. I received two postcards a few days apart. The first one was a picture of the Great Pyramid against the sky, which (if I hadn't known better) I could have assumed to be 10 feet high. The second card showed a camel at the base of the Pyramid, clearing up any doubts as to its size.

In Show Magazine, we once did an issue on the theme of Beauty. There were hundreds of pictures around the office relating to our topic: people, paintings, architecture, movie stars, real stars, furniture, automobiles, machines, jewels. By some strange coincidence, three pictures came to lie side by side on the table. One was taken by an electron microscope of a human cell a thousandth of an inch in diameter; next to it was an image of a Jackson Pollock painting six feet wide; and the third was a photograph taken at Mt. Palomar Observatory of a galaxy billions of miles across. The three photographs looked almost identical; they had the

A human motor cell, magnified 280 times.

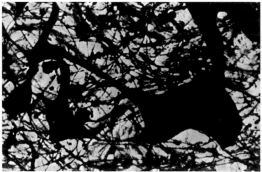

A detail of a Jackson Pollock painting.

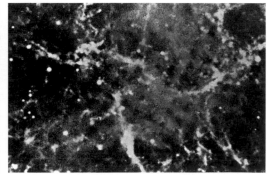

A distant galaxy billions of miles across.

same pattern but no scale. Placing two subjects beside each other in the wrong size relationship creates a disturbing image. Magritte painted an apple that filled a room. In Jean Vigo's film, Zero for Conduct, people change size in relation to their varying importance to a schoolboy.

A scene from Zero for Conduct.

At its extremes, scale is always interesting. The Eiffel Tower quickly became one of the wonders of the world. Miniature doll houses, complete with table settings and chairs less than an inch high, fascinate children and collectors alike. A painting done on the head of a pin and the Golden Gate Bridge each stimulate the curiosity of the beholder. Edward Albee's play, Tiny Alice, takes place in an elaborate room in which there is a model of the entire house set on a table. At one point a fire breaks out in the model, leaving the audience in doubt as to whether the room on stage is only part of a larger model.

The idea of scale as attention grabber is obviously anything but new. The Pyramids mentioned earlier are some of the oldest artifacts of Western civilization. The Colossus of Rhodes and the enormous hand and foot at the Roman Campidoglio are other examples. What becomes interesting is placing two objects together which are in extreme contrast. A fashion photographer once balanced a tiny red shoe on a finger of the giant hand in Rome.

We photographed the Bugatti Royale, the largest passenger automobile ever built, with a little girl sitting on the running board. Charles Eames begins his great short film, Powers of Ten, with a couple picnicking in the park, and then zooms out into space, so that the area of the picture increases by the power of ten with each frame. In relatively few moves, the image encompasses the whole galaxy. He then shifts into reverse, back to the picnic. The possibilities are endless.

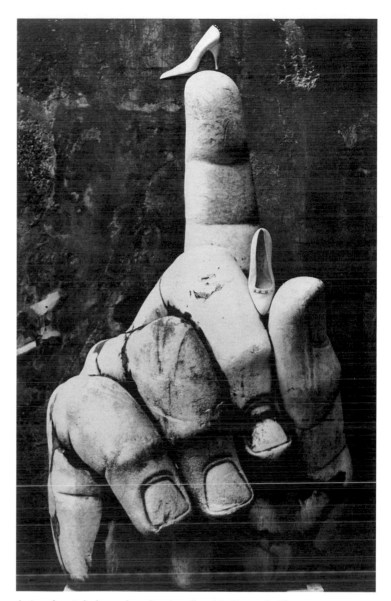

A tiny shoe is balanced on the giant hand in Rome for Vogue.

Climbing up Lincoln's nose on Borglum's Mt. Rushmore Memorial.

A proposed cover for
<u>Fortune</u> Magazine whose
cover line was
"The Re-lighting of Philip Morris."

A proposed cover for
<u>Vanity Fair</u>, playing
on the optical illusion
that the candle flame
and the moon can be
of equal size
in certain circumstances.

Some of us have mor

The ad agency Ally & Gargano's
campaign for Karastan carpets.
Four foot wide model rooms were built.
The birds and the props were
photographed to scale, and in
perspective, and were then inserted
as silhouette prints into the models.
The entire room was then reshot with
a large camera.
Tom Wolsey was Art Director.

inely developed nesting instincts than others.

INVEST IN

A proposed cover
for <u>Vanity Fair</u>.
The empty room was built
on a stage and was photographed
showing the empty frame.
The same room was then decorated
1900's style, photographed
in perspective and inserted
into the frame.

An ad for Olivetti.
The theme is
"Olivetti <u>is</u> the office."
The box was built
to the scale of
the typewriter.
The light fixture is a
ping pong ball and the
door knob is a push pin.

A poster for Simpson Paper.
The theme was "Connections,"
and I chose the connection
to yourself.

Three solutions that use
a variation of the same idea.

The first is AIGA's
1983 Call for Entries.

Business Solutions,
a computer magazine,
shows a man in a museum
of obsolete objects.

Finally, the headline
in this ad for
five typewriters is
"The Olivetti Collection."

7
Type as Design

I think of type as the bridge between word and picture. Abstract shapes in the form of single letters combine to make words, and words conjure up imagery. Type can function as design in two ways. The first is where the letter forms themselves become illustrative elements. Early books used illuminated initials; the title page of Shakespeare's First Folio, the Gutenberg Bible, the Book of Hours. Or, type can assume literal meaning as imagery. On the book jacket shown (p.74), the second 'O' in the word "moon" becomes a representation of the moon.

These images differ greatly from person to person. I look at the word "war" in print, and it brings back images that I actually saw during World War II. What pictures appear to someone who has never seen war? I once gave a lecture addressing this idea, that a three-letter word can generate so many images, and called it "A word is worth a thousand pictures."

On returning from a visit to Jerusalem, I described that fabled city in a letter to a friend who had never been there. As I wrote, I wondered what imagery my words would create in her mind. Would this added information about Jerusalem change the stereotypes she had already formed from reading other words and seeing other pictures?

I have always believed that designers who cannot express themselves in words cannot be very good at designing either. They certainly would not make good art directors, because an art director has to be able to convey—in words written or spoken—the content and mood of an assignment to another artist for execution. In explaining the assignment, he should also consider the bias that artist will bring to it, and fit his description around those perceived prejudices.

Reading, especially early on in life, trains you to be able to translate imaginatively from word to picture. Sitting in your room reading A Passage to India is a much more participatory and creative activity than watching the movie, which forces the director's particular translation, brilliant as it may be, onto every viewer. I am afraid that television, which now does this translation for most children for many hours each day, may be responsible in two or

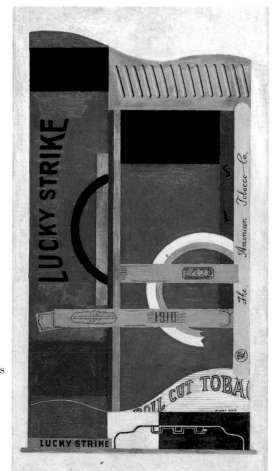

Stuart Davis.
Lucky Strike, 1921.

Davis often used commercial products as the subject of his paintings, including the typography on their packages and in the ads promoting their sale.

three generations for a severe shortage of adults with the ability to make these translations with any individuality.

Sometimes type itself can also become the design, the illustration, or can, by its physical aspect, reinforce the literal message. Who hasn't wondered at the beauty of Japanese calligraphy—or even the Japanese type forms in a booklet for Honda? Because most of us are unable to read the message, we see the beauty of its abstract design without distraction.

In this century, Western poets like Apollinaire or Christian Morgenstern or e. e. cummings used typographic forms as pictorial elements to complement their writing. I have always loved a design solution where the visual aspect of the type itself acquires literal meaning. Type reaches its highest potential when doing double duty.

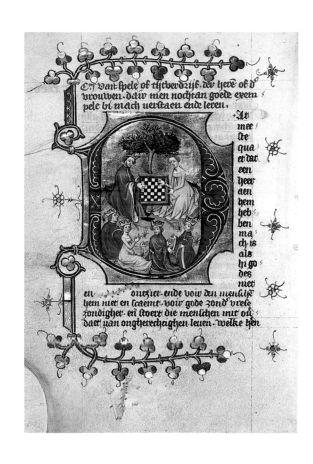

Initial letters intricately illuminated were the illustrations on medieval manuscript pages, such as this one from around 1405. I used the same idea on a title page in 1957.

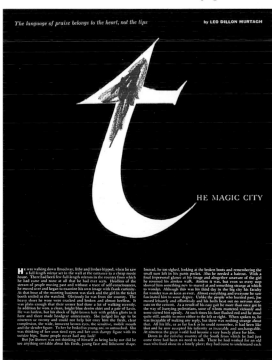

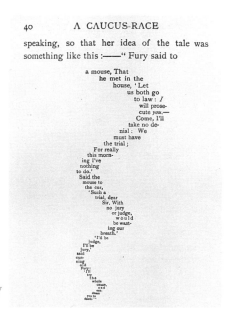

Lewis Carroll, in <u>Alice in Wonderland</u>, let the shape of the typography help tell the story.

69

34 NEW
SCHEMES FOR
THE SOUTH

LATE NEWS
FOR LEGS:
THE
SHIMMERING
STOCKINGS

GIFTS: THE
THOUGHT IS
THE THING

DECEMBER 1959
60 CENTS

Two <u>Harper's Bazaar</u> covers where Richard Avedon's photographs are combined with storytelling type.

60 Cents
December 1958

There was no retouching done to this illustration for an article on travel to the Orient. The only light source was the Japanese letter, which became a true reflection in the eye.

Two pages from <u>Bazaar</u>.
The type becomes
a tennis net, and
then a cone of light.

A poster for a type house.
The photograph of the
Pitti Palace in Florence
had been taken years earlier.

JULY 1984

PM Typography
2513 So. Winchester Blvd., Campbell, CA 95008
(408) 374-0743

Printing: B&C Lithographers, Santa Clara, CA
Designed for PM Typography by: Henry Wolf, New York
Display Font: Visual Graphics Corp.
Typeface: ITC Kabel
Plates & Film: Eastman Kodak Co.
Paper: Cross Siclare's Larius Brillante & Mohawk's Superfine

S	M	T	W	T	F	S
1	2	3	4	5	6	7
8	9	10	11	12	13	14
15	16	17	18	19	20	21
22	23	24	25	26	27	28
29	30	31				

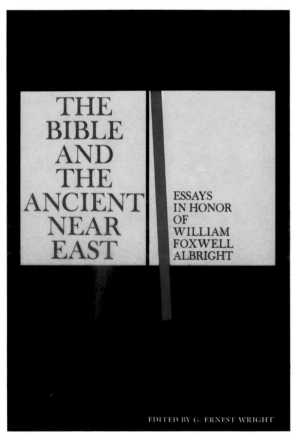

THE
BIBLE
AND
THE
ANCIENT
NEAR
EAST

ESSAYS
IN HONOR
OF
WILLIAM
FOXWELL
ALBRIGHT

EDITED BY G. ERNEST WRIGHT

Three book jackets where
type becomes the illustration:
the "O" as the moon,
the book as a book cover,
and the "O" as hidden treasure.

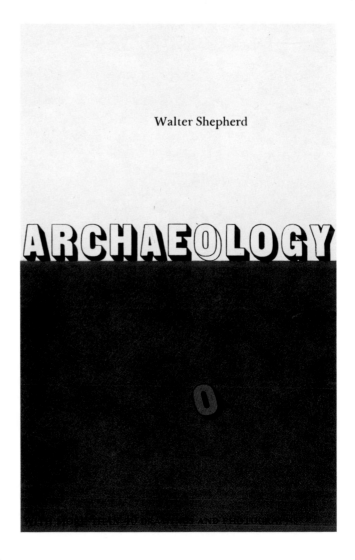

BIG

9 BIG RACES EVERY DAY

A poster for the
Aqueduct Racetrack, which
is known as the Big A.
The "A" becomes
the starting gate.

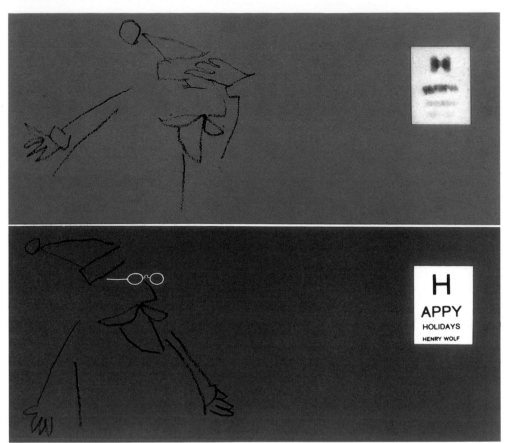

A Christmas card
I designed for myself.
The nearsighted Santa
sees the eye chart
in focus after he
puts on his eyeglasses.

Two stories on
related subjects that
ran side by side
in Bazaar.
The typography was
an adaptation of an
illuminated manuscript.

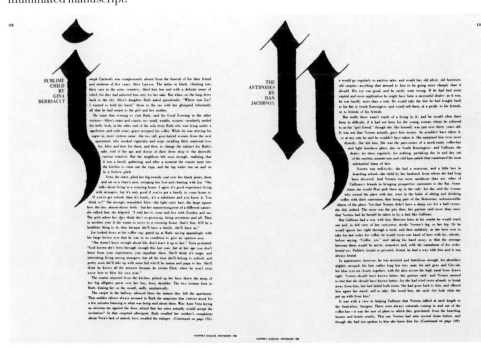

A logo for a promotion called "Details" at Burdines department store. The word was assembled from accessories such as buttons and zippers.

A cover of
<u>Dial</u> Magazine whose
theme was television's
role in the elections.

A cover for the Swiss annual, <u>Photographis</u>. This is one of my photo-homages to Magritte.

Giardini di Montecatini: Paradise Regained

Even 2400 years ago, in Italy, there was a fast lane. And the world's most privileged people found an antidote to it in a way no pill or seven-mile-run has ever equalled.

Princess Marcella Borghese experienced this antidote in the ancient gardens of Montecatini, in Italy's Tuscan hills. And blessedly, she reintroduces it to the modern world.

Giardini di Montecatini is a glorious body, bath and fragrance collection based upon the ancient precedent that scent can change the way you feel.

The collection includes five therapies for your bath, for your skin, for the air around you.

Each sublimely sensual therapy will sweep away the clutter of contemporary life, to lift you up, calm you down.

Welcome to the Gardens of Montecatini.

You've never been anywhere like it before.

PRINCESS MARCELLA BORGHESE

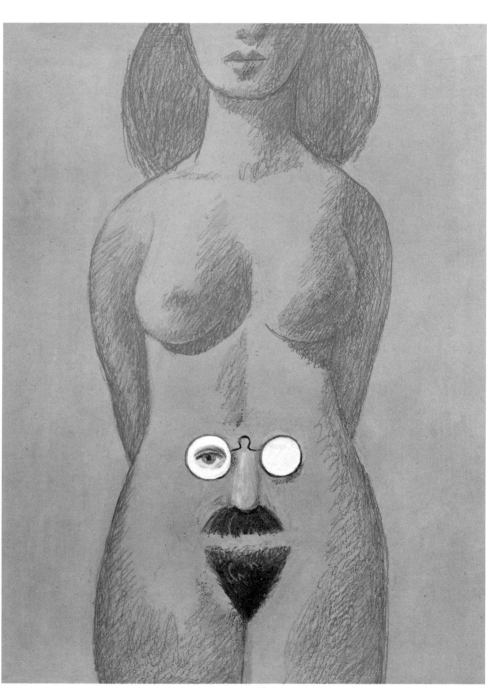

A cover for a book on Psychoanalysis.

9
Color

When my sister and I were old enough to be invited out to dinner, my father's advice was "don't eat anything gray." Color has an immediate visual impact on our senses. Man Ray knew this when he created his blue bread and, later, a Spanish-born artist named Miralda capitalized on the same idea by serving black potato salad at his parties. Our associations between color and emotion are very deeply grounded. In Western culture, white is pure and black is evil, red means passion and green signifies hope. Blue skies are happy and gray skies sad. There is a psychological test where the subject is asked to combine two colors from many very scientifically selected swatches, in order of preference. The test claims to be able to separate people into several groups related to basic character traits.

In a passage dealing with the Spanish kings, a historian wrote that the Habsburg colors (which happened to be black and yellow) were perfectly suited to the Spanish court life with its deadly formality (black) and pervasive jealousies (yellow). Climate and geography have a lot to do with color preference. The brilliant reds, yellows and pinks of Mexican folk art must come from early visual experiences, which have little in common with those of a child growing up in foggy, gray northern Norway. As a result, the colors in Rufino Tamayo's paintings bear no resemblance to those in the works of Edvard Munch.

As with any deep-rooted emotion, the artist can very effectively work with it or against it. Some artists oppose their heritage and disown tradition, almost as if they were ashamed of it. Others make it their lifelong subject. Chagall, in 70 or more years of painting, never strayed very far from his Russian Jewish background in either color or story line. Malevich, another Russian

Man Ray: Blue Bred (Pain Peint), 1966.

Changing the color of an everyday food is both shocking and funny. The pun also works in the title in two languages.

living around the same time, denied both the sentimentality and the colors traditionally associated with his background.

Besides evoking mood, color in imagery has other qualities. Cool colors like blue and green recede, while reds and yellows come forward. Albers, in his paintings of rectangles and squares, alters both mood and distance by changing the colors of identical shapes.

Monochromatic palettes are often very beautiful and may be easier to handle than a full range. Picasso, early on, went through a "blue" and "rose" period before allowing himself a full palette. And then in <u>Guernica</u>, when the subject demanded it, he left out color altogether. Black-and-white photography is appealing because in a medium where the artist cannot control color as effectively as a painter can, omitting it can sometimes be more beautiful. Black-and-white is an abstraction; no one has ever seen anything in black and white. For this reason black and white images have a compelling effect. The colorization of the great films of the thirties is a terrible blunder committed in the name of updating. In reality it is more like downgrading these classics.

Kasimir Malevich.
Suprematist Composition: White on White, 1918 (?).

The denial of color.

Photographic film is balanced for either indoor or outdoor light. When both are present, strange colors result as in this picture of a Paris bakery.

An advertisement for Karastan rugs implying that nature is not perfect because sheep don't come in a variety of colors.

A cover for a book on color,
where the tube of paint becomes
the subject of a painting.

A fashion feature on red dresses.
Since we painted the piano,
it couldn't be returned to
the store that had loaned it to us.

An interpretation of
Alban Berg's opera, <u>Lulu</u>,
done for WNET.

A Paris evening, 1959.

This cover of <u>Holiday</u> Magazine
was done for an issue featuring
the Caribbean. The girl was shot in
black and white, and the color
in the fruit and sky
was painted onto the print.

90

HOLIDAY

NOVEMBER 1968   75c

10 Collage

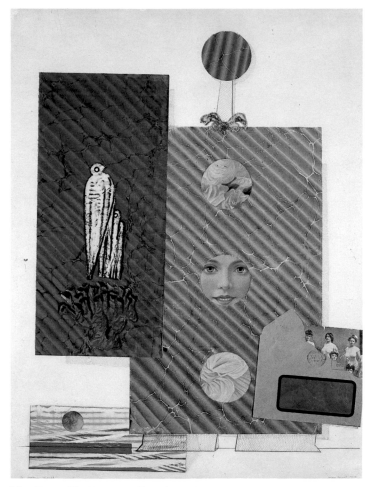

Max Ernst. The Postman Cheval, 1932.

An extensive scrap file, a sense of humor,
a large dose of fantasy and a talent for design
are the ingredients of a successful collage.

As I have previously mentioned, techniques
for making memorable imagery often overlap.
This is especially true with "Collage" and
"Unexpected Combinations," but there are
also some differences. In "Unexpected Combinations," the images are often created by
combining two photographs or two or more
drawings of the artist's own making. Typically
in collage, the images are not "made" by the
artist but are "found" pictures; photographs
clipped from magazines, parts of advertise-
ments, old engravings or rubber stamps.

A talent for drawing, painting or photography is
not absolutely necessary for making a successful collage. The artist in this medium is above
all a good editor, a pack rat and a paste-up man
with a sense of design. It helps to have col-
lected visual oddities of all kinds over the
years. Tram tickets from Barcelona, calling
cards from Japan, illustrations clipped from a
Sears and Roebuck catalog of 1920 are examples of valuable ingredients. By judiciously
combining several of these images in a seemingly haphazard way, you can convey a message, a feeling, a mood. Often the strange
juxtaposition of unrelated pictures from widely
different sources can create a startling effect,
not only because of the variety of literal content, but by the great range in style and technique displayed.

In the best examples of this genre, the artist
combines found images with some drawing or
painting of his own, which helps to unify the
often strange mélange. Robert Rauschenberg

László Moholy Nagy. <u>Chute</u>, 1923.

The artist combines photography, air brush and pen-and-ink drawing.

and Larry Rivers have used this method with great success, sometimes even including three-dimensional objects in their assemblages. Joseph Cornell's work is comprised mainly of three-dimensional objects. He combines things like glass beads, doll house furniture and old engravings in his wonderful boxes.

In spite of its seemingly unrelated sources, a successful collage makes a definite point and relates to a theme. The painter James Rosenquist, who was trained as an outdoor poster artist, goes a step further. Instead of assembling found images, he enlarges them tremendously, combines them and then renders them on canvas as a realistic painting. The effect is one of a combination of billboards.

The danger in the collage method is that the end result can look more like a scrapbook than a piece of design or a work of art. The selection of the ingredients, their placement, the contrast between the different surfaces, the size and color relationships are as crucial to the success of the work as when imagery is created by the artist from scratch. It is a little like baking a cake. The ingredients may all be first-rate, but if they are not combined in the proper order or in proper amounts, the result may be inedible.

Collage requires ingenuity, a vision that includes a sense of humor and a real understanding of the subject matter to be illustrated. The line between a run-of-the-mill album page and a successful assemblage of images, which together make a point, is often a very fine one.

Cover and back cover of a self-promotion brochure.

The first cover of <u>Show</u> Magazine. The numeral "one"
was combined with symbols for the contents within.

An <u>Esquire</u> feature for
which four advertising agencies
were asked to prepare a hypothetical
advertising campaign for
Senator Kennedy's bid for
the Presidency.

Repackaging **TED**

As Seen By Trahey/Wolf Advertising

Be my Partner

Be my Partner

Be my Partner

Be My Partner: One half is always Ted.
The other half changes:

Posters.
Quick flipping
TV commercials.

Possible variation
"Be My Better Half"
"One Man Can't Do It Alone"

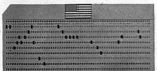

DEPARTMENT OF OPINION

ELECTED

DRAFTED

WANTED

A button for all seasons.

Knocking the opposition:
As always at the beginning,
we plan to go light on this,
both in volume and in tone.

The Telegram:
At an important turning point of the campaign, Senator Kennedy
makes his big promise: "If elected, I shall send, on the day
of taking office, the following telegram...."

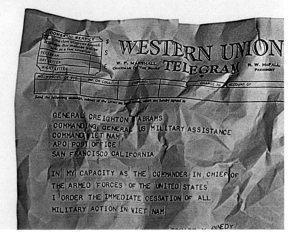

WESTERN UNION TELEGRAM

GENERAL CREIGHTON ABRAMS
COMMANDING GENERAL US MILITARY ASSISTANCE
COMMAND VIET NAM
APO POST OFFICE
SAN FRANCISCO CALIFORNIA

IN MY CAPACITY AS THE COMMANDER IN CHIEF OF
THE ARMED FORCES OF THE UNITED STATES
I ORDER THE IMMEDIATE CESSATION OF ALL
MILITARY ACTION IN VIET NAM

SHOW

THE
MAGAZINE
OF
THE
PERFORMING
ARTS

$1.00
OCTOBER 1961

1

THE BEST THEATRE
WEST OF BROADWAY

ORCHESTRA

SEPT
16
1961

SATURDAY EVE

EST. PRICE $8.26
FED. TAX .73
N. Y. C. TAX .41

TOTAL
$9.40

A 108

GOOD ONLY
SATDAY EVE
SEPT

ORCHESTRA
16
1961

$9.40

An ad for Kohler
bathroom fixtures.
The hands hold
the products as though
they were jewels.

THE BOLD LOOK
OF **KOHLER**

European styling and Kohler quality join hands. The Chardonnay™ pedestal lavatory in Raspberry Puree™,
available in fourteen other decorator colors. Other custom faucets also available. For more details see the Yellow
Pages for a Kohler showroom, or send $2 for a color catalog to Kohler Co., Dept. AD4, Kohler, Wisconsin 53044.
C-5011 Copyright 1985 Kohler Co.

ULTIMA II I

Revlon's Ultima II introduction of a new line of sun care products.

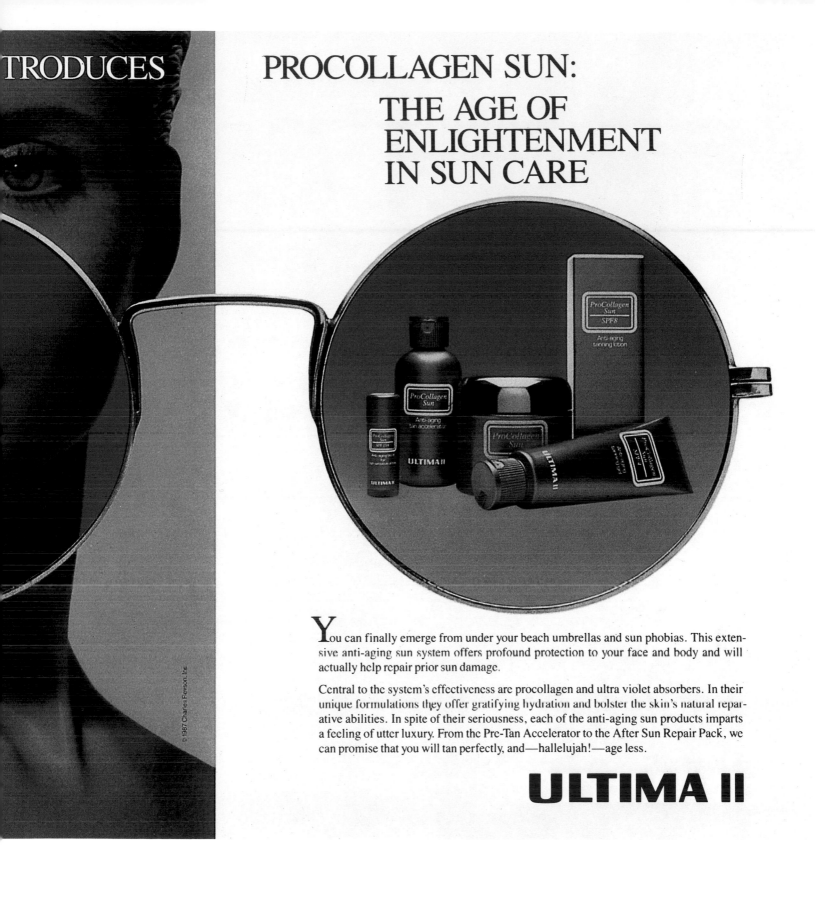

Four treatments of the box:
two are book jackets,
one is a cover for
B.F. Goodrich's
in-house magazine,
and the last is
a poster for IBM's
Christmas television
special.

BFGToday

August/September 1977   Volume 1, Number 3

Creativity:
blasting loose with new ideas

Plus... How is BFG doing?
Thomas and Ong give
a candid assessment

THE FUTURE
OF
ARCHITECTURE

FRANK
LLOYD
WRIGHT

Henry Wolf

PROFUSELY ILLUSTRATED

Mikhail Baryshnikov's
the NUTCRACKER
The dazzling
American Ballet Theatre
production starring
Mikhail Baryshnikov
and
Gelsey Kirkland
Wednesday, Dec. 24
8:30-10 P.M. (EST)
CBS-TV
Best holiday wishes
IBM

11
Improbable Settings

In the late 1950s, the tracks of New York's Third Avenue elevated trains were torn down, and many turn-of-the-century, four-story brownstones were wrecked to make way for new office buildings. One old brick wall was left exposed, showing decades of stained wallpapers in Mondrian-like juxtaposition, and in a bathroom on the third floor a tub was still securely fastened to the wall. An enterprising photographer and a courageous model collaborated to create a wonderfully surprising picture —a nude standing upright in the tub 40 feet above the ground against the background of Manhattan. What made this image memorable was the uniqueness of the situation: an ordinary scene of a girl in a tub had been transported into a totally improbable setting.

Perhaps this new technique originated as an antidote to the "keeping up with the Joneses" attitude that prevailed in advertising and editorial imagery for decades. Cadillac cars were always pictured against marble mansions with chauffeurs at the ready, and the fashionable ladies in <u>Vogue</u> and <u>Town & Country</u> were photographed in their Park Avenue drawing rooms filled with overstuffed chintz sofas.

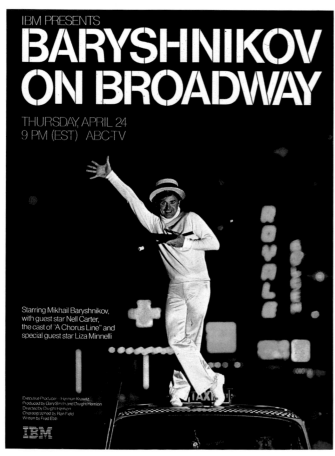

A poster for an
IBM television special.
The great dancer performed
on top of a taxicab
in 20° weather.

Buster Keaton, comic genius of silent films,
stranded near an arctic subway station.

Eventually the search for a new approach made photographers abandon these realistic, but usually upscale, background settings. Subjects were instead placed in surprising and often jarring surroundings. A great innovator named Martin Munkacsi, a native of Hungary who worked in Berlin in the twenties and thirties, was brought over by Hearst as a star photographer for Harper's Bazaar. He quickly became a favorite of movie celebrities like Marlene Dietrich. Munkacsi pioneered the idea of motion instead of the frozen poses that had been commonplace. He was also instrumental in bringing about the transition from stilted settings resembling department store windows to much simpler surroundings. When the background was not to his liking, he carried a roll of white paper that was unfurled behind the model to hide lamps, chair legs and extension cords. To the best of my knowledge, he was the first photographer to use this portable, no-background device, which every photographer in the world now considers standard equipment.

Munkacsi may have provided the transition from crowded living room settings, or studios with draped white plaster columns, to experimentation with real-life backgrounds. Fashion pages began to show models in evening dresses photographed in garage elevators, electric power plants, and on oil storage tanks at the Esso refinery. Expensive jewelry, which had been traditionally photographed against a velvet background, was suddenly being placed on black rocks, rubber floor mats or sheets of reflective plastic.

I accompanied Richard Avedon on a location trip to Cape Canaveral (as it was called then), where he photographed fashion pages for Bazaar with the Apollo IX rocket as background. Scale was a player in these pictures, but it was the strangeness of the setting that made them memorable.

As with every new movement, improbable settings were often carried too far, with the emphasis placed purely on effect. The best examples demonstrate a surprising counterpoint between subject and surrounding.

Henri Rousseau. The Dream, 1910.

The nude transposed into a lush jungle, couch and all.

Erwin Blumenfeld. Sur la Tour Eiffel, 1938.

The great model Lisa Fonssagrives daringly floats over Paris.

In these two fashion ads, a dress model appears to be walking on water and a shoe model is submerged underwater. Both were photographed exactly as they appear.

Any Palizzio is better than no Palizzio

SHOES & HANDBAGS

A portrait of Time Magazine art critic Robert Hughes being bombarded by masterpieces from the Museum of Modern Art.

"Don't turn
historic landmarks
into parking lots":
A public service ad
for Xerox Corporation.

From a brochure
for a real estate firm:
Illustration for
the theme
"Manhattan High Life."

An illustration in <u>Esquire</u> of a model lost in a department store.

12
Humor

It is very difficult for the single image to be funny. Traditionally, a joke has two phases: there is a long build-up to create, and reinforce, an expectation in the listener or viewer, and then the quick destruction of that expectation. The more convincing the build-up and the more instantaneous the destruction, the louder the laugh. Early filmmaking depended heavily on the sight gag. Charlie Chaplin leans nonchalantly against a living room wall; the wall collapses backward and Chaplin slides into a lake. Robert Benchley is lecturing on taxation in double-talk. The window behind his desk reveals a view of the Capitol, and the spectator's expectation is of a high-level official in his Washington office. The paper shade on the window snaps and the view changes to an alley replete with garbage cans (the Capitol was only printed on the shade). In both examples, a series of images create a scenario which is then blown to pieces.

In a single still image, humor depends heavily on the cooperation of the viewer, who fills in the rest of the joke. Some photographers have consistently been able to do this well. Robert Doisneau took the famous picture of a married couple looking into an antique store window filled with small objects. The husband is sneaking a glance at a painting of a nude lady in one corner. Elliott Erwitt is another photographer who distills humor from a single photo, often by depicting ludicrous situations such as a picture of a statue of Diana whose arrow is aimed at an unsuspecting visitor. Duane Michals, who realized the difficulty of capturing humor (or tragedy) in one frame, perfected a technique whereby the story is told in several sequential frames—a sort of combination of Muybridge's motion studies and comic strips.

Humor is playing an increasingly important role in advertising, particularly television commercials. These are basically 30-second movies, and are therefore not restricted by either lack of motion or by the limitations of the single image. The repetition used in successful advertising is made bearable through use of humor. The danger is that if the joke is too good, consumers may remember the joke but not the sponsor.

Robert Doisneau's photo of the loyal wife with her sly husband and the unsuspecting victim in Elliot Erwitt's museum shot (left) make the most of comic situations where the participants are unaware of what's going on.

Charlie Chaplin's genius in finding the perfect balance between funny and sad has never been equalled. Here he is in <u>Gold Rush</u>.

Humor is often a by-product of surprise or shock, and can therefore be found in "Unexpected Combinations" or "Improbable Settings." M*A*S*H's 4077th Unit worries about sex and bathtub gin to keep war and death from prevailing. This is humorous because of the unlikely setting and because poking fun at our government is sacrilegious. It's similar to defacing the Mona Lisa: the idol or the totem destroyed makes us laugh unexpectedly.

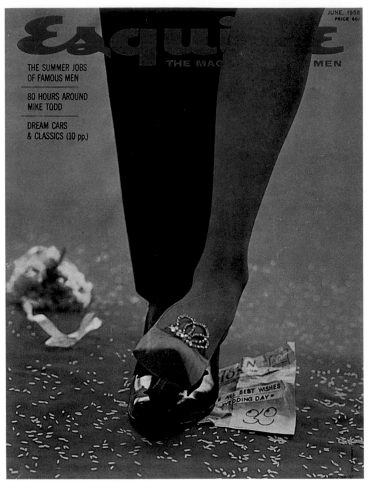

An <u>Esquire</u> cover for June which is, of course,
the traditional month for weddings.

A "recession" Thanksgiving dinner, 1974.

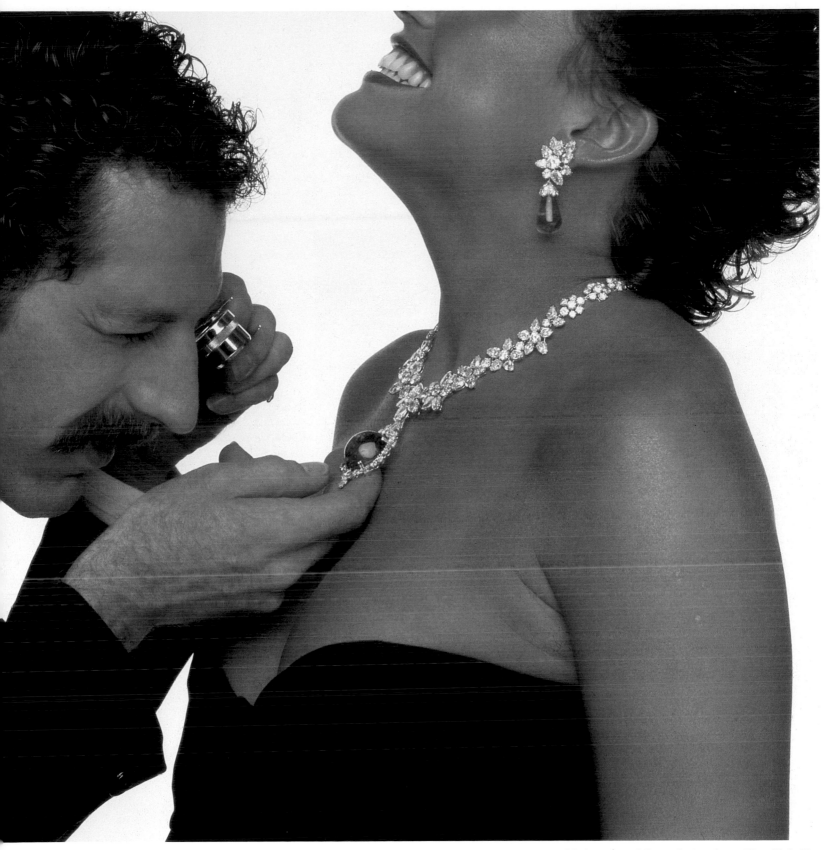

From a <u>Town and Country</u> portfolio on the jewelers of New York City.

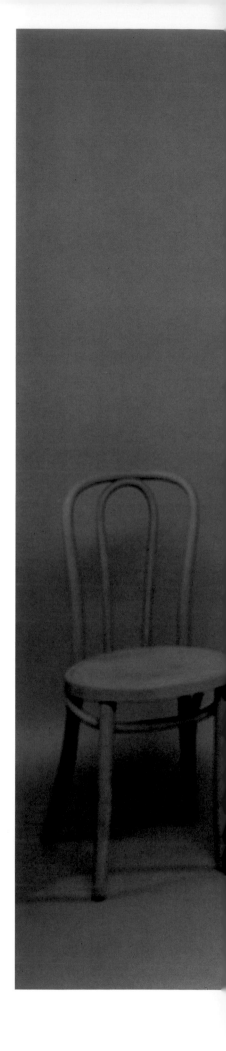

An illustration for a
<u>New West</u> Magazine story
about an imaginary religion,
in which the Triscuit
is the Holy Wafer.

A spread in <u>Esquire</u> on eating kosher. The Orthodox Jew is turning his back on pork chops and milk.

A <u>New York</u> Magazine cover
for a lead article
entitled "Enclosed Encounters."

Humor by contrast:
The beauty with the lush
blonde hair and the
bald-headed man. From
an editorial page on
hair care in <u>Cosmopolitan</u>.

A cover for <u>Photographis</u>: film becomes fashion.

A proposed cover
for an <u>American Photographer</u>
issue on humor.

This view of Christmas
for an <u>Esquire</u> title page
was very unpopular with
the ad sales department.

My own stationery.
When opened, the letter
looks like it had already
been thrown away.

13 The Object

The next five chapters are an important afterthought. I could not identify overall techniques to group them sensibly, and yet they present subjects that most imagery is made of. Each poses special opportunities, unique problems and restrictions. In many of the examples, techniques previously examined play important (but not starring) roles.

Cézanne was too shy to paint directly from the nude model, so he often worked from photographs. He turned the living subject into a still life he could contemplate at will, without intrusion. The still life affords a leisurely approach; you don't have to deal with people's mood swings under changing circumstances. The painter Morandi spent most of his life working from a collection of jugs and bottles, which he painted and drew in ever-changing combinations.

Henri Cartier-Bresson. Paris, 1932.

A photo which could not be arranged. Unlike a still life, it only "existed" for fragments of a second.

The beauty of working with objects is the luxury of doing it at leisure without the pressures of photojournalism. Cartier-Bresson's book The Decisive Moment, contains wonderful photographs that could only have been taken at a particular point in time—not a second earlier or later. This is one reason photojournalism could not be included in this book, because an identifiable technique for making reportage more interesting doesn't exist.

Fascination with the object may be a question of personality. It seems ideally suited to the artist/photographer who has difficulty dealing with people, and who loves the introspective activity of contemplating an object. Irving Penn, a great photographer whose still life pictures remain unsurpassed, has done much fashion photography in which the model is as carefully arranged and designed in the space as a still life. Bill Brandt did wonderful sculptural nudes, which to me look more monumental and immovable than a much heavier object would. Picasso, a mercurial extrovert, was able to switch easily between still life and figure.

2 Strange Perspective

Bill Brandt. Nude, Belgravia, London, 1951.

In his wonderfully distorted nudes,
the English photographer creates space
and a cool separateness.

One of the simplest ploys for making imagery
exciting is to see things from a strange vantage
point or in an unusually distorted way.

Perspective is a convention, a means of
creating the illusion of a third dimension on
a two-dimensional surface (a drawing, an
architectural rendering, a painting or a photograph). The viewer collaborates to create the
illusion of distance on a flat plane.

"Normal" perspective can be defined as an
approximation of what the eye sees when the
observer is in a standing position. You can easily depart from this norm by placing yourself in
a position that is less common: a room viewed
with one's head flat on the floor, a figure seen
from directly overhead, a landscape from
a plane 30,000 feet up, or the earth from a
moon rocket.

Any change from the view we are most accus-
tomed to is immediately compelling, because it
is not what we see most of the time.

Depth perception is created by the fact that
we have two eyes. When we look at our watch,
the angle of the sight lines between our two eyes
is more acute than when we look at the moon.

Irving Penn. After-Dinner Games.

In every art form, there are masterpieces. Penn's still-life photographs have not been equalled either in their attention to detail or their technical perfection.

In studio photography, still life provides the opportunity to try another version the next day: lights can be shifted, the camera can be moved, the arrangement can be changed. There is no weather to worry about and no model fees. All you may have to do is replace a faded flower or a glass of champagne gone flat.

There are two basic ingredients in a still life, object and arrangement. Objects have to be selected both for their beauty and their meaning. Then they must be properly placed to design the photograph. The next step is to light the arrangement, and to look at it not just with your eyes but through the camera's eye, which changes and distorts the image in many ways. Using a large format camera, you see the image upside down in the ground glass, which is the reason why many photographers (including this writer) suffer from stiff necks.

Photography, unlike painting or writing, can never start at zero with the blank canvas or the blank page. I love still life because it is the closest you can come to having total control over the finished work.

Title page for an article on cooking with eggs in House Beautiful.

This ad for
Van Cleef & Arpels shows
$6,000,000 worth of rings.

An ad for a perfume called
"Ma Griffe,"
which means "my signature."

ma griffe is my signature

MA GRIFFE IN PERFUME,
EAU DE COLOGNE,
SAVON, PARFUM CREME.

JEWELS BY
VAN CLEEF & ARPELS.

THE GREAT CRAFTSMEN

The creation
of unique,
expensive,
handmade and
beautiful objects
survives
brilliantly,
if precariously,
in odd corners
of Europe.
The pride and
love involved in
their making is
prodigious, and
their fame is
out of all
proportion to
their total number.
Photographs
and Text
by Henry Wolf

MARANELLO, ITALY: FERRARI
In 18 years of production, the Ferrari has become the most sought-after performance automobile in the world. Enzo Ferrari, now 65, an ex-racing driver, produces 600 of them a year. They are made by hand, each part being lovingly fashioned from the raw steel. Ferrari races his cars as a matter of pride—and to test their design. In a brief decade and a half, they have won more competitions than any other make in all the history of the automobile.

Ferrari automobiles and
Patek Philippe watches
are illustrated as part
of a <u>Show</u> Magazine essay
on world class products
and their designers.

A title page in <u>Esquire</u>
for a portfolio
on classic automobiles.

THE
AUTOMOBILE'S
CLASSIC
DECADES:
A
PORTFOLIO
BY
LESLIE SAALBURG

THINGS

Two spreads
from a prototype
for <u>Class</u> Magazine
concerned with
the best of everything.

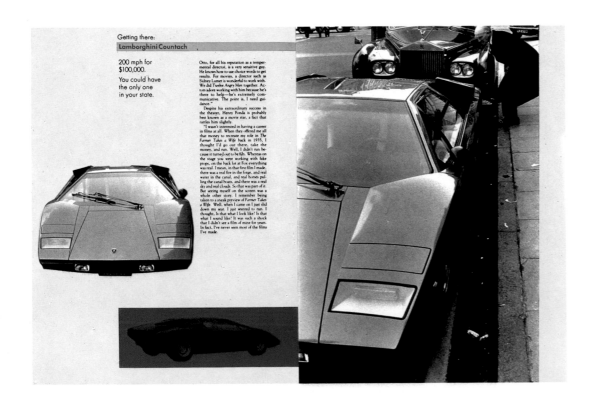

Mead Paper asked several
photographers to interpret
the theme
"Good Morning America."
I had one side of
the glasses mirrored to
reflect an orange sunrise.

Three still lifes from
<u>McCall's</u>,
<u>Bride's</u> Magazine
and <u>House Beautiful</u>.

126

14
Fashion and Beauty

A cover for a fragrance catalog.

Sometime in 1959, I had the wonderful experience of attending an "opening" fashion show at the House of Balenciaga in Paris. Balenciaga was to fashion design as Ferrari is to aficionados of automobiles. He was a genius of the highest order. I was new to the world of fashion and was never really moved by it, always claiming that a girl with a great smile wearing a potato sack is more attractive than a bored sophisticate in Dior's greatest evening dress. (This dismayed my editors at <u>Harper's Bazaar</u> greatly.) That afternoon at Balenciaga, I saw fashion as art. He designed a coat, not to be sold to just any customer, but made for one particular woman. He constructed it like a piece of moving architecture. This coat, which came to a point in the back that touched the floor, would break its straight line when that woman walked, to keep time with the rhythm of her steps. The front brim of her hat would move up and down, simply because it was so light that air currents caused it to be in constant motion.

Unfortunately, this kind of couture is all but gone now—it was only affordable for a wealthy few. Fashion, however, has never been more in the news and in the foreground, constantly reported in the media, its influence everywhere. Mass-produced goods reflect its current edicts. Instead of Balenciaga's one-of-a-kind dresses, designers such as Cardin distribute and license their creations around the world. Belts, towels, stationery and chocolates bear their initials and so command high prices. Ralph Lauren has made a fortune by reviving a look that was fashionable in England 50 years ago.

Nowhere is the influence of fantasy, and the pressure to be new and different, as intense as in the little fraternity producing the images that sell fashion in the pages of magazines. Skirt lengths or the number of buttons on a suit are not news items of great significance. Therefore, the presentation, the quality of the photograph itself, has to make up for this shortcoming. Fashion photography has produced some of the most innovative, strange, and, on occasion, trend setting images. In any given month, dozens of magazines show the same suits, dresses and coats. It is the interpretation, the background against which they are shown, that makes them seem more desirable in one magazine than another. Fashion is never at rest. As soon as an era creates its own vague ideal of beauty, forces rise to rebel against it and make lies out of yesterday's truths.

In recent years, the arts, traditionally the haven of beauty, have become more interested in its opposite. Techniques for making movies and ads have become so slick that attempts to be innovative by being less technically correct, or to shock by using deliberate ugliness, are commonplace.

The fashion gurus, the beauty experts and the cosmetics companies are constantly claiming to have found an Ideal Beauty. Beauty, however, is like love: too much acquiescence breeds skepticism and too much pursuit, retreat. The true test always comes in retrospect. We judge beauty mainly after the fact, by what has survived.

Richard Avedon.
Jean Shrimpton in Space Suit, 1965.

Avedon's genius comes partly from being exactly in step with the times. Here, in collaboration with the art director Ruth Ansel, he marked the beginning of the space age on a cover of Harper's Bazaar.

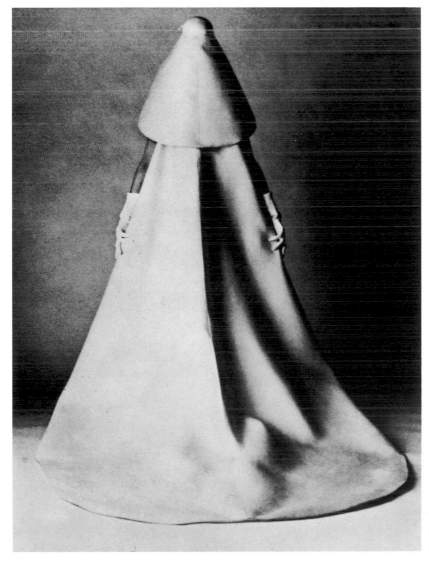

David Bailey. Balenciaga Great Coat.

The Spanish-born designer was an architect, a sculptor of clothes. He was able to bring a monumental quality to his fashion designs.

129

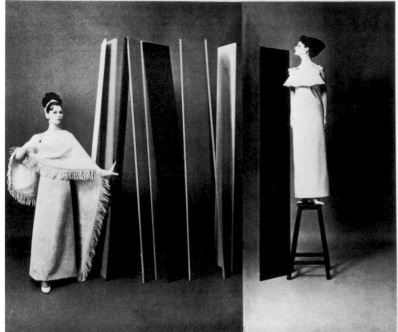

Three spreads from
<u>Harper's Bazaar</u>
all done around 1960.
The top and bottom
shots were taken
at the Paris collections.

PARIS DRESSES: STRAIGHT AND FRINGED

PARIS REPORT

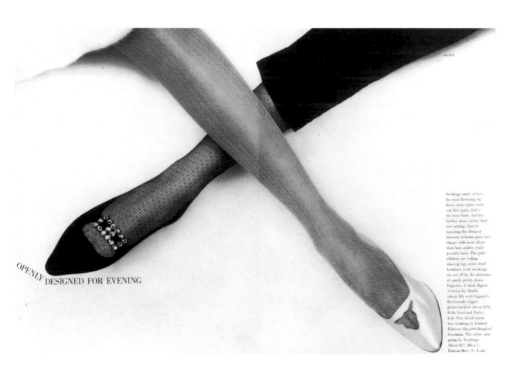

OPENLY DESIGNED FOR EVENING

night drama:
organdie cape,
squared train

An ad for Yardley lipsticks.
The model's head was
photographed through a
diffusing filter
to give it a soft quality.

I. Magnin and Saks Fifth Avenue experimented with the concept of catalog-as-magazine. The idea was fun but short lived; unfortunately, this amusing way of showing fashion could not substitute for hard sell.

From a story in <u>Town & Country</u> on photographers and their favorite models, here are Janice Dickinson and Horst.

An illustration for an article in <u>McCall's</u> about beautiful hair.

STRAIGHTENING OUT HAIR PROBLEMS

Healthy hair depends on a healthy scalp, and by far the most common scalp affliction is seborrhea—just plain dandruff. The condition is apparently hereditary, and there is no cure—but frequent washing with shampoo formulated to combat dandruff will keep scaliness to a minimum. Dandruff, by the way, doesn't mean you have a dry scalp. Dandruff can occur whether your scalp is dry or oily; in either case, shampoo frequently—every day, if you like. If scalp is dry, compensate with a conditioner to keep hair manageable. If dandruff shampoo doesn't control the problem, see a dermatologist.

Hair loss is something that worries many women. Although thinning hair is inevitable in old age, women of all ages sometimes notice small bald patches. The condition is called alopecia areata, and, since it often coincides with periods of emotional stress, it's thought to be psychogenic. There's no remedy for it (except getting enough sleep and trying to keep calm), and it usually disappears as mysteriously as it came. Best advice: If bald spots appear and then go away, simply ignore them. However, if the condition persists, if spots grow larger and more widespread, consult a doctor. It is medically treatable.

Severe hair loss, although common in men, does occur occasionally in women, particularly women with a family history of male baldness. It's associated with an imbalance of male and female hormones and may occur in women only after menopause, when estrogen levels have dropped. Some doctors think estrogen-replacement therapy may /turn to page 122

90 McCALL'S, JANUARY 1976

HENRY WOLF

An ad for Elizabeth Arden's mango colored lipstick.

From a Saks Fifth Avenue promotion. The models were photographed in an Art Deco apartment.

A cover of <u>Dial</u> Magazine recreating the magic of dancing in Harlem during the '30s.

NOT EVERY WOMAN CAN WEAR RED

GEOFFREY BEENE

Red Parfum and Eau de Toilette from the Geoffrey Beene Fragrance Collection.

Two ads for fragrances by Geoffrey Beene. They were intended to face each other in a double page spread. Unfortunately, "Red" was an unsuccessful product,

GREY FLANNEL *suits any man*

but "Grey Flannel" is still going strong years later.

15
Sex and Romance

From the 1934 Oscar-winning film
<u>It Happened One Night</u>:
Claudette Colbert and Clark Gable
had to be separated by
a hanging blanket
so they could share a motel room.

When the Hays office reigned as the self-appointed censor and moral arbiter of Hollywood films, a man and a woman, even if married, could not be shown sleeping in the same bed. Nowadays it seems that a film without sexual scenes, nudity, and a torrent of words that would have made James Joyce and Henry Miller blush, is not promotable. This enormous change in the code over the last four decades may have opened the doors to a new era of realism, but it also removed an ingredient that has been a mainspring of artistic activity since the beginning of time. Sex has shock value, and writers and image makers have used wonderful ingenuity to challenge and circumvent its taboo.

The newsstands are crowded with magazines containing endlessly varied photographs of genitalia in sharp detail, and films try hard to deserve the X-rating necessary for commercial success. Our current no-holds-barred attitude has created the need for a new potential to shock. Violence, slashed faces bleeding to death on ghetto sidewalks, bodies blown to bits on Vietnam battlefields or the disemboweled figures in Francis Bacon's paintings all explore this possibility, which has not yet reached its zenith. On the other end of the spectrum, as a reaction to so much explicit sex and violence,

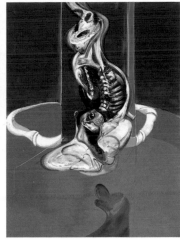

Francis Bacon.
Three Studies for a Crucifixion, March 1962.

The great British artist explores the last taboo:
gore and violence.

there is a marked return to old-fashioned romance. It may be coincidence that our hearts-and-flowers revival started during the presidency of an ex-Hollywood actor nostalgic for the America of the thirties and forties. When Myrna Loy, William Powell and Cary Grant were role models, they charmed with innuendo rather than fact.

The ups and downs of permissiveness and censorship are nothing new. Roman orgies gave way to witch hunts and inquisitions. The sexual freedom of the English Restoration deteriorated in less than half a century into the depths of Victorian prudishness, when postcards showing a lady's leg were sold as illegal pornography.

In the advertising annuals of 40 years ago, a smiling, wholesome girl, sometimes showing just a little cleavage, sells everything from lipstick to typewriters. The sexual revolution and Women's Liberation have put a stop to all this. One says it's no longer enough; the other that it's exploitative.

Yet in one form or another, sex and romance are going to survive, both in real life and as subject matter for imagery. They are, no matter how influenced and distorted by fashion and morality, among the constants of civilization.

An ad for a boutique
in the late 60's,
featuring leather,
metal and bondage.
The New York Times
refused to run it.

143

A cover for <u>New York</u> Magazine feature on "Togetherness."

A test shot of an aspiring model wearing a 1920's dress I had bought at the Paris flea market.

An illustration for an _Esquire_ story on bubble gum wrapper collecting.

Another fashion illustration done for <u>Esquire</u>.

A photograph for <u>Ski</u> Magazine. I enjoyed the assignment, even though the illustration was never printed.

Experiments done for a prospective book on nudes.

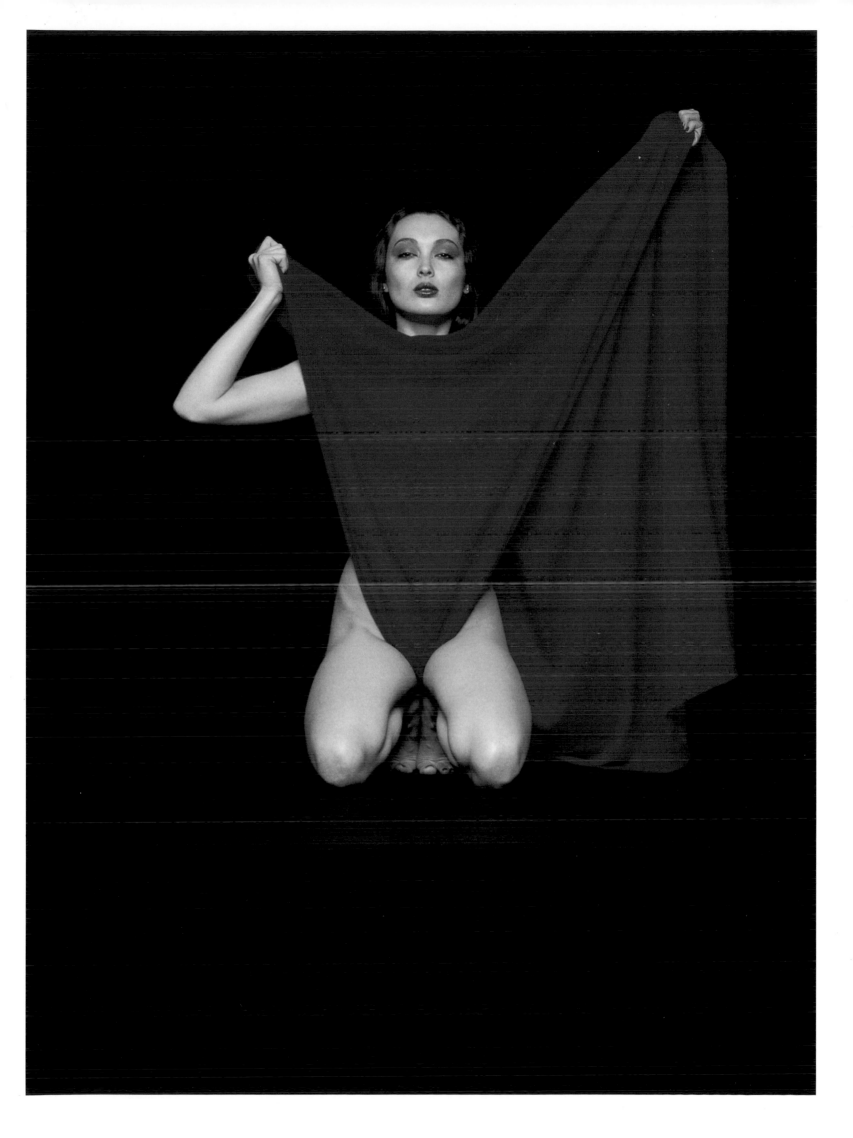

16
Roundabout Ways of Telling a Story

Making imagery "talk" is the hardest method to define. It borrows from "Humor," "Unexpected Combinations" and "Manipulated Symbols," yet has a life all its own. Its main operative mechanism is the use of pictorial metaphor, which becomes an illustrated pun. George Lois once did a controversial <u>Esquire</u> cover on the masculinizing of American women, which showed a beautiful girl all lathered up for shaving. In one of the great posters done for Dubonnet, the French apéritif, the artist A. M. Cassandre illustrated a three-part play on words: the first, "Dubo," meaning something beautiful, the second "Dubon," meaning something good, and finally the entire name, "Dubonnet." I was once asked to do a logo for the Men's Store at Bergdorf Goodman. My solution, which did not take much work on my part, was to simply emphasize the last three letters.

The first time this sort of approach appeared in my work is an important milestone in my checkered career, because the assignment was so important to me. The solution came after long evenings of agonizing, and many false starts. The director of the American Institute of Graphic Arts had asked me to do a poster for their first paperback cover show. I came up with dozens of sketches involving stacks of

A cover for <u>Time</u> on the oil crisis.

books, bookmarks, type, eyeglasses and endless combinations thereof. I decided that none were usable and they weren't. The next afternoon the director called me and said that the deadline had passed and could I please send my poster. I started to apologize, saying that my solutions were not good enough to use. She was obviously upset by this, and asked what the paperback show was supposed to do now, only she pronounced it "paper...back," as two words. A photograph of the back of a rider in Vienna's Spanish Riding School (from an <u>Esquire</u> story photographed earlier) was lying on my desk. As she said "paper back," I was looking at the photograph, and within a second the solution presented itself. I put down the phone, punched a hole in the back of the rider and folded the torn paper forward, got back on the phone and told the director that the poster would be over in the morning. There are few thrills comparable to the sudden flash that occurs after long hours of self-doubt and indecision.

This technique is often useful when the straight story is difficult to take, indelicate or simply not beautiful. A fashion magazine once gave me the assignment of illustrating hair loss in women. The straight approach, which I often call the "tomato red solution" (red being the first thing you think of when you hear the word "tomato"), would have been to take a portrait of a balding woman. To avoid this depressing prospect, I came up with the idea of a close-up shot showing hair left on a comb—an allusion to hair loss rather than a confrontation with it. Another problematic assignment was an ad for a girdle. I decided to photograph a nude with a dotted line drawn on her hip, delineating the outline she would prefer to have.

A few years ago, IBM wanted to run an ad dramatizing the benefits of hiring the handicapped. The approach they decided on, in conjunction with both the agency and a courageous employee, was to photograph one of their managers who had lost an arm in Vietnam holding his calling card in his mechanical hand.

Making a point indirectly can often be more poignant, humorous or memorable than in the obvious way. The ingenuity used to get around a bare fact can result in a surprising image that has never been used in that context.

A. M. Cassandre, possibly the greatest of the French poster artists, combined words and pictures to tell the story.

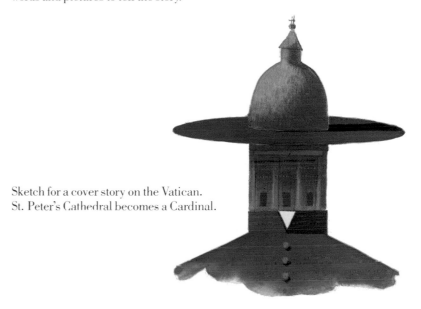

Sketch for a cover story on the Vatican. St. Peter's Cathedral becomes a Cardinal.

For a cover of <u>New York</u> Magazine, an illustration on Downward Mobility.

A girdle ad that promised
the wearer a slimmer hip.
The model is drawing
the outline she'd like to have.

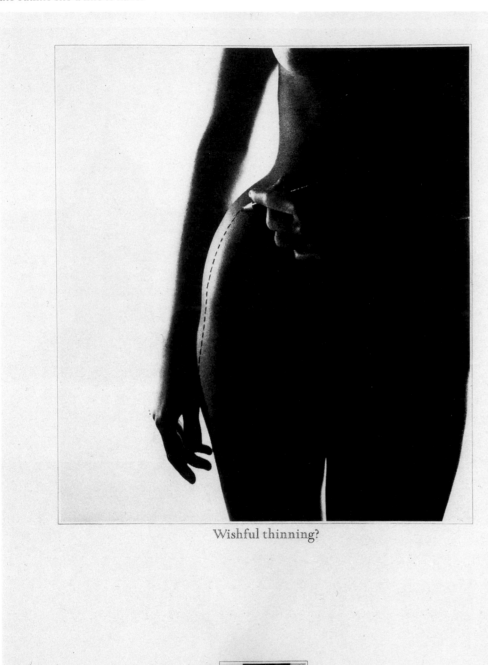

Wishful thinning?

Enhance by Lily of France

This ad for IBM
promoted the hiring
of disabled persons.

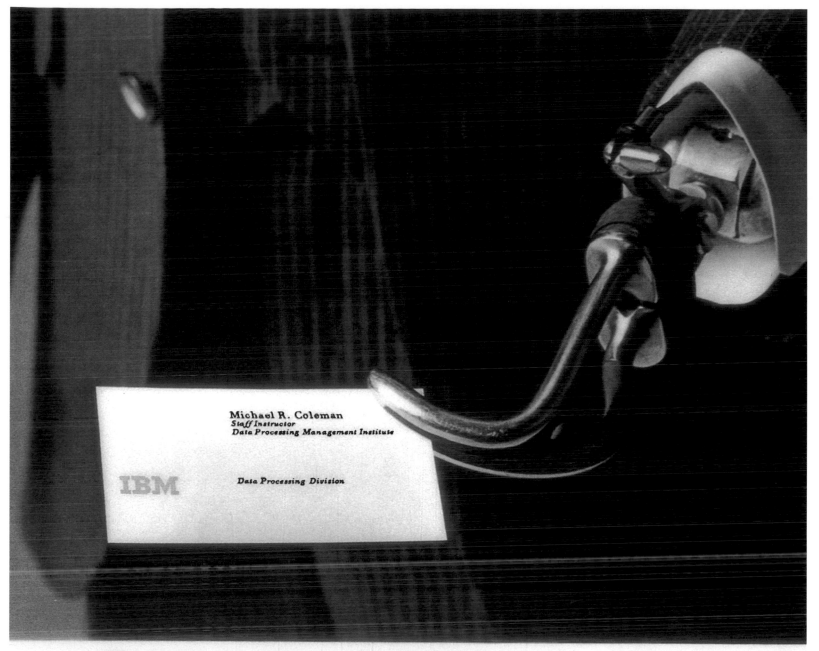

The man behind this hand is Michael Coleman.

The company behind this man is IBM.

There's a story behind both of them.

After the Marines and Vietnam, Coleman earned his MBA and began selling computers for IBM. Promotion followed promotion, and he now teaches our customers how to get the most out of their computers.

His success doesn't surprise us. People with disabilities keep proving that they are as capable as other workers. As reliable. As ambitious. And just as likely to succeed.

At IBM the proof is everywhere, in every part of our business.

The same is true at other companies.

Yet, some people just won't believe that the disabled can do the job. It has to make you wonder who's handicapped.

And who isn't. **IBM**®

My illustration for a
<u>Woman's Day</u> article
about hair loss.

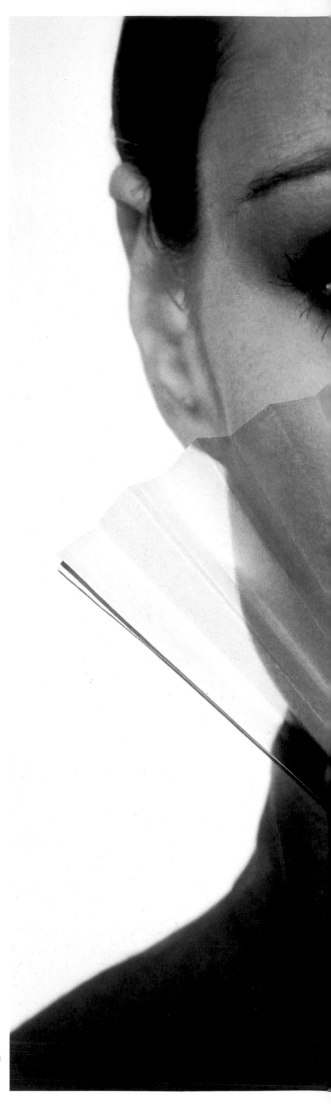

For a <u>McCall's</u> story on
facial wrinkles, this photograph
was projected onto
the fan and then reshot.

A proposed cover for a "Fortune 500" issue listing the 500 largest U.S. corporations.

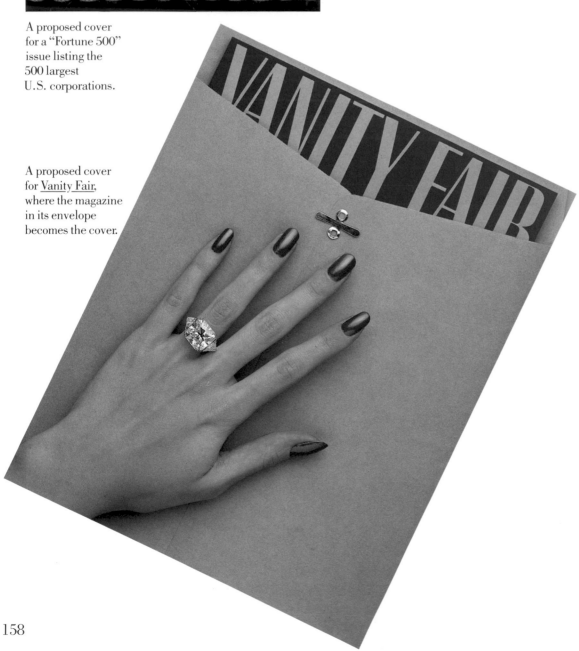

A proposed cover for <u>Vanity Fair</u>, where the magazine in its envelope becomes the cover.

158

A cover for <u>Dial</u> referring to Carl Sagan's article on "Who Owns Outer Space?"

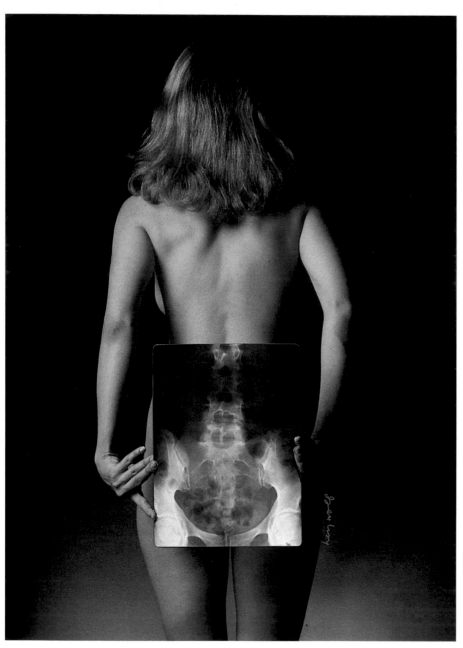

A <u>Time</u> cover whose lead story was about the all-American backache.

This poster was done for the AIGA's first paperback book cover show.

PAPERBACKS U. S. A.: An Exhibition of Covers: 1957-1959

PAPERBACKS

17 Celebrity

The overture to a musical or an operetta has a very definite and important function. When you hear the melody again in the body of the work, it already sounds vaguely familiar, and you are ready to accept it or even love it. The power of this mental preconditioning, or déjà entendu, is enormous. It is also closely related to a phenomenon that we are concerned with here: the previously seen image, the recognizable face. The impact of celebrity and the power of fame are direct results of the power of déjà vu.

When I was a young boy in France, on an afternoon when there was no school I went to see a film called Test Pilot, starring Clark Gable as a devil-may-care flyer complete with white silk scarf, goggles and a crooked smile. For days after, I tried to walk and hold my head like Gable, and thought I had succeeded until I saw my reflection in the dark glass of a store window.

The exploitation of this force, of this desire to be like a celebrity, is one of the oldest mainstays of advertising. The movie star with the gorgeous smile uses a certain toothpaste, and the implication is quick and deadly: the lady on the bus who sees the ad connects the toothpaste with acquiring a great smile of her own. The fact that the lady may have buck teeth, or

that the model may have gone through much make-up and the photograph much retouching is unimportant.

The power of the persuasion lies in the assumption—wrong as it may be—that a photograph doesn't lie. The basic supposition that the subject must have been in front of the camera is primarily responsible. Any manipulations, such as make-up, optical distortion, soft focus lenses and retouching, are overshadowed by the fervent belief that a product can imbue the viewer with some of the glamour of the model used in the picture. It isn't simply that the physical look is worth emulating. Seeing the famous face immediately sets into motion a veritable chain reaction of legends and misconceptions about the celebrity.

Many years ago, the advertising agency in which I was a partner created a campaign for Blackglama Mink with the slogan "What Becomes A Legend Most." The idea was to show famous female personalities wearing a mink coat without mentioning their names. The criterion was, of course, that they be instantly recognizable. The campaign is still being run, I believe, by the successor to our agency. It must be increasingly difficult to find the right faces for such a long-running ad campaign. Real legends like Marlene Dietrich,

Marlene Dietrich in <u>The Blue Angel</u> (1930) and in a Blackgama mink ad (1969).

WHAT BECOMES A LEGEND MOST?

An exquisite extra-dark natural mink heard only by the Great Lakes Mink Man. BLACKGLAMA

Clark Gable, Myrna Loy and Spencer Tracy in <u>Test Pilot</u>.

Joan Crawford or Judy Garland have earned their esteem through years of continuous achievement and exposure. The studio system that produced film stars of Greta Garbo's magnitude has given way to more fragmented production arrangements and a faster rate of obsolescence.

It is hard to think of 50 faces today that would be instantly identifiable around the world. There is also an increasing desire for privacy that keeps a world-famous face like Woody Allen's from being exploited by publicity, which studios demanded the right to use for their own purposes in the glory days of Hollywood. In addition, a better understanding by the public that celebrities aren't always what they're cracked up to be, and that behind the famous facades often lie troubled, insecure human beings, probably undermines the power of fame as a sales tool. There are also regulations and controls that now make some claims like "Doctors prefer Camels" illegal. Still, images recognizable by millions, and the aura that goes with their story, surround us via interview shows, magazine stories, ads and television commercials. Celebrities often make more money from this secondary phenomenon than from their profession—whether actors, singers, or golf champions.

The brilliant Woody Allen, who has become a celebrity in spite of himself.

Elizabeth Ashley captured
in a Beverly Hills Hotel
bathtub in 1963.

Raquel Welch and friend.

Henry Fonda
in the studio
shortly after making
his last film.

A 1959 portrait of
Buster Keaton, taken at the
St. Lazare train station
in Paris.

Enzo Ferrari in his factory.
I asked him to dream about
his next racing engine.

Brooke Shields during
a sitting for Clairol,
when she was around
eight years old.

How to buy jeans.

Brooke Shields 12 years later.
Carol Channing with
a girl's best friend.
Lauren Hutton in the same
Ogilvy & Mather campaign
for American Express.

How to buy a diamond.

How to buy a camera.

Duke Ellington at the keyboard.
He would not accept a fee,
but asked instead that
a hundred typewriters be sent
to a needy school in the South.

Duke Ellington at the keyboard.   olivetti's studio 45: the Brightwriter

George Balanchine's world is bounded by

George Balanchine
and his ballerinas,
taken for <u>Show</u> Magazine.
The difficult part
of this assignment was
convincing him to appear
<u>under</u> the dancers.

Michihiko Oka (left)
and Judith Jamison,
both of the Alvin Ailey
American Dance Theater.

Lena Horne on a <u>Show</u> cover illustrating a story called "Breaking the White Barrier."

SHOW

THE
MAGAZINE
OF
THE
ARTS
_____
75 CENTS
SEPTEMBER 1963

BREAKING
THE WHITE
BARRIER:
LENA HORNE
SPEAKS
ON THE ARTIST
AND THE
NEGRO REVOLT

Meryl Streep in a
photograph used to
advertise Robert Benton's
<u>Still of the Night</u>.
In the film,
she watches a murderer
through a crack in the door.

A few years ago, in one of my classes on graphic design, I gave a strange but interesting assignment. The students were to read Tolstoy's War and Peace, and then write a scenario transposing the basic story line into present-day America. Many attempts resulted, ranging from unsuccessful to disastrous. One of the more memorable ones (because it was the most ludicrous) had Pierre cast as an insurance salesman for Metropolitan Life in Chicago, and

Vienna, 1930.

Looking Back

On the Promenade des Anglais in Nice, France, with my family. Winter 1940.

Natasha as a trainee for the Horn and Hardart restaurant chain. The important lesson taught by the inherent lack of success in this exercise was to understand the importance of background. War and Peace needs the uniforms, the horses, the balls, the duels, the devoted servants, the large estates and the Russian winters. Story line can rarely be divorced from background or transported into a different time.

An artist's style is largely a function of his own background. You can be obsessed with your past or rebel against it. Early memories often become your yardstick for what things should look like. In spite of having spent 40 years in America, a window for me is still one that swings out, as in Austria and France, rather than the American version that slides up and down. In this lifetime, I will not consider a digital timepiece a "real" watch, and the 1937 Cord automobile, which I fell in love with as an 11 year old, will remain for me the quintessential car. J. S. Bach grew up in a family of musicians and heard music played daily as an infant. It was natural that he became a composer, and many other members of his family also grew up to become musicians. I am sure that my early surroundings have a great deal to do with the direction my work has taken.

I was born in Vienna in 1925, a city with an illustrious past, diminished by the aftermath of

With the Army of Occupation in Japan, 1945, using my first camera.

My grandmother
with her two daughters.
Vienna, 1900.

With my mother in
New York, 1982.

The family house in Vienna, 1935.

defeat in the First World War. The old order that had been in place for centuries was badly shaken, but still very much in evidence. My parents were a living bridge between the pre- and post-war worlds. Three generations of our large family lived in a house built in the 1860 s by a great-uncle. My father and the other children played on its big staircase around the turn of the century. The walls were three feet thick, and when I was little I was afraid of the dark spaces between the double doors. Every Sunday night there was a dinner for at least 20 family members. The maids who worked for my three great-uncles across the hall were related to our cook. On Saturdays my sister, my cousins and I would have lunch with our uncles, and when we came back our clothes would be aired out on the balcony to get rid of the smell of their Havana cigars.

For the first 13 years of my life, I wore tailor-made suits and high-laced shoes. On Wednesdays a lady came who was supposed to teach us French, but we taught her gin rummy instead. When we moved to France some years later, we did know how to count to 100 in the language.

It was a secure and orderly childhood, and I am sure that my longing for this sense of order still shows up in my work. In designing a page, I often choose to place things centered and head on, almost two-dimensionally. I achieve depth by placing one thing behind another, rather than by perspective. This may be my method of covering up the disturbing underside I must have sensed under all that apparent perfection in my childhood. Sigmund Freud was still alive and well then.

This old world sort of life came to an abrupt end in 1938. Hitler occupied Austria, and it soon became clear that, being Jewish, we could not stay in Vienna. A three-year odyssey through France and North Africa followed. I attended many different schools for only months at a time. After an uneasy period of hiding from the Germans, and two detention camps in Morocco, we finally managed to evade the Nazis again. Due to tireless interventions by my uncle in New York, we arrived at the Hoboken docks during Christmas week, 1941. Pearl Harbor had happened while we were crossing the Atlantic on a slow Portuguese steamer. New Yorkers were crazily blacking out windows, newly at war. There was a great wave of patriotism to be felt everywhere.

For the first time in three years, we had all the food we wanted. We lived in a small furnished apartment on the West Side of Manhattan, and I attended the School of Industrial Arts on West 40th Street. Frank Sinatra was singing at the Paramount Theater a few blocks up. The size and bustle of New York, the new language, the lack of friends was overwhelming. I was quiet, skinny and shy. My cousin said I always looked at my shoes instead of straight ahead. The week after I turned 18, I registered for the draft, neglecting to mention that I had contracted malaria in Africa.

After graduation in June, and a summer job putting watchbands on watches for $22 a week, I was inducted into the army in October, 1943. For the first time since Vienna, I felt I belonged. I gained 20 pounds and started looking straight ahead. After several months in New Guinea, and landings on Leyte and Luzon, our division ended up in Japan a few weeks after Hiroshima. The four months I spent there were some of the happiest of my life. I had survived the war, we were out of danger, there was a strange country to be explored, and the wonderful expectation of returning to New York.

The studio on 73rd Street, Manhattan.

The country house. North Salem, New York.

In my office at <u>Esquire</u>, 1956.

A note from Harvey Schmidt.

Portrait with Esquire Mask.

With Suzy Parker in Paris, 1959.

Note from Diana Vreeland,
fashion editor of <u>Harper's Bazaar</u>.

In March, 1946, I started working in a two-man art studio on West 74th Street and going to school at night. After a few years at a small advertising agency, I started as a designer at <u>Esquire</u> Magazine. I became art director a few months later, mainly because of Arnold Gingrich, a wonderful man who was the founding editor of the publication. Arnold referred to me as his 27-year-old art director during my entire tenure. Becoming restless, I moved to <u>Harper's Bazaar</u> in 1958, where I was lucky to work with Nancy White and Diana Vreeland. They tried to incorporate me into the fashion world, but to this day I don't understand it too well. Mrs. Vreeland considered that shortcoming an asset. I worked long and hard during those years, got married and divorced, smoked Camels without filters and wore black neckties like Arnold Gingrich.

The late, great Bill Bernbach was once asked by a friend why he never tried to get me to work at Doyle Dane Bernbach, and he allegedly replied: "Anything Henry touches turns to elegance and we don't want it."

In 1961, I was offered the chance to start a new magazine for the performing arts called <u>Show</u>. It was a period of my life when my professional and social activities completely overlapped, and I enjoyed myself tremendously. <u>Show</u>, dur-

On assignment in Jamaica, 1967.

Envelope for a bill from Tomi Ungerer.

With H.R.H. Prince Philip,
Duke of Edinburgh.
at the Bi-Centennial dinner
for the Benjamin Franklin
Fellows of the Royal Society of Arts.

ROYAL SOCIETY
FOR THE ENCOURAGEMENT OF ARTS
MANUFACTURES & COMMERCE
LONDON

PRESIDENT: HIS ROYAL HIGHNESS THE PRINCE PHILIP, DUKE OF EDINBURGH, K.G., K.T.

This is to certify that

Henry Wolf

has this day been elected a

BENJAMIN FRANKLIN FELLOW

of the Royal Society for the Encouragement of Arts,

Manufactures and Commerce

12th October 1970
Secretary

At a costume party
around 1970.

The Gold Medal of the AIGA, 1976.

The Art Directors Club
Hall of Fame Medal, 1980.

179

In the art department at Show Magazine, 1962.

With Ivan Chermayeff in Aspen, 1969. We were co-chairmen of the International Design Conference.

Sitting on the status symbol, a middle-age folly, 1982.

ing its short life span, became the last opulent American magazine. In 1963 I bought a house in the country that started as a small farm, and which I am still renovating 24 years later. After Show (having run out of magazines), I went to work for McCann-Erickson whose Chairman, Paul Foley, became another great mentor. He approached advertising the way he did everything else—with humor, modesty and style. I worked on Alka-Seltzer, Buick, Aqueduct Race Track, Coca-Cola, Geigy and other accounts. In presentations, my concepts were the far-out ones, and there was always a "safe" campaign to fall back on in case the client fainted. Sometimes, by a strange quirk, my ideas made it.

In 1966 I felt confident enough to become part owner of a small agency. My partner Jane Trahey and I had six years of fun, and created some wonderful ads for a lot of fashion clients —Bill Blass, Trigère, Blackglama, Danskin— but also for Union Carbide and Olivetti. I did my own photography and learned "on the job." In 1972 I went into business for myself. I was lucky to meet another great lady, Doris Shaw, who was the Advertising Director at Saks Fifth Avenue, and for many years I did much of their work. We more or less invented the catalog-as-magazine, which became widely imitated throughout the retail industry.

New York had changed by the seventies, as all America had been changed by Vietnam. I started wearing eyeglasses full time and bought the building on the East Side where I still live and work. It's convenient in snowstorms (but the lack of exercise makes you gain weight). I have always been a little behind my time, but eventually I started doing television and some film. A great variety of advertising assignments came my way, and even occasional design projects: House Beautiful Magazine, Sesame Street and the original Dial for Public Broadcasting. There were a few years of consulting for IBM on entertainment projects; house organs for B.F. Goodrich, RCA, Champion Paper, VanCleef and Arpels; covers for Time and a recent consulting job for Revlon. Just this afternoon, I received two phone calls within an hour of each other, both asking me to design a book. Sometimes I think it's been a good run, and it doesn't look as if it's over yet.

One of the many paintings done in the last eight years.

With Gina Lollobrigida, 1957.

With the model Mya, 1980.

Acknowledgments

5   Photo Günter Knop

9   Photo Sam Antupit

11   Henry VIII. Detail of painting by Hans Eworth (after Holbein). The Bettmann Archive

     Antonio Stradivari. Violin, 1691. © 1979. The Metropolitan Museum of Art, New York, Gift of George Gould, 1955. 55.86

13   J.A.D. Ingres. The Comtesse d'Haussonville, 1845. Oil on canvas. © The Frick Collection, New York

     René Magritte. The False Mirror, 1928. Oil on canvas, 21¼ × 31⅞ in. Collection The Museum of Modern Art, New York. Purchase

     Harry Callahan. Eleanor, 1953. Photograph. © Harry Callahan, Courtesy Pace/MacGill Gallery

14   Un chien andalou. Luis Buñuel, 1924. Courtesy The Museum of Modern Art Film Stills Archive

     Meret Oppenheim. Object, 1936. Fur-covered cup, saucer, and spoon; cup 4⅜ in. diameter; saucer 9⅜ in. diameter; spoon 8 in. long; overall height 2⅞ in. Collection The Museum of Modern Art, New York. Purchase

15   American Photographer

16   Courtesy Money Magazine

17   Esquire. Photo Somoroff

18,19 Chermayeff & Geismar, Xerox

20   New York, Holiday

21   Ogden Corporation

22   © 1959 The Hearst Corporation. Courtesy Harper's Bazaar. Photo Ben Rose

23   © 1987 Charles Revson, Inc.

24   Bill Brandt. Nude, Belgravia, London, 1951. Photograph. © Bill Brandt/Photo Researchers

25   Giorgio de Chirico. Gare Montparnasse (The Melancholy of Departure), 1914. Oil on canvas, 55⅛ × 6⅝ in. Collection The Museum of Modern Art, New York. Gift of James Thrall Soby

     The Nymph of the Lo River. Chinese painting, Southern Sung Dynasty. Illustration of poem by Ts'ao chih. Section of handscroll, silk makimono, 122⅛ × 9½ in. Courtesy the Freer Gallery of Art, Smithsonian Institution, Washington, D.C.

26   Elizabeth Arden

27   The Dial

28   Herman Miller, Inc.

29   American Photographer

30   IBM

31   Rochester Institute of Technology

32   Bergdorf Goodman

33   Andy Warhol. Green Coca-Cola Bottles, 1962. Oil on canvas. 82½ × 57 in. Collection Whitney Museum of American Art. Purchased with funds from the Friends of the Whitney Museum of American Art. 68.25

     A Night at the Opera, 1935. Courtesy The Museum of Modern Art Film Stills Archive

34   Graphis

35   Esquire

36   Kohler Co.

     © 1977 Princess Marcella Borghese, Inc.

37   © 1959 The Hearst Corporation. Courtesy Harper's Bazaar. Photo Derujinsky

38   Show

39   Show. Photo Sokolsky

40   Jacques-Henri Lartigue. Grand Prix of the Automobile Club of France, 1912. Photograph. Collection the author. Courtesy the Association des Amis de Jacques-Henri Lartigue

41   Marcel Duchamp. Nude Descending a Staircase #2, 1912. Oil on canvas. Approx. 58 × 35 in. Philadelphia Museum of Art (Louise and Walter Arensberg Collection)

     Eliot Elisofon. Marcel Duchamp, 1952. Eliot Elisofon, Life Magazine, © 1952, 1980, Time Inc.

     Eadweard Muybridge. From Animal Locomotion, 1887. Photograph (Collotype). Collection the author

     Champion Paper

42   © 1958 The Hearst Corporation. Courtesy Harper's Bazaar. Photo Fonssagrives

43   © 1978 The Hearst Corporation. Courtesy House Beautiful

44   Show. Photo Hiro

     Columbia Pictures. Photo Mark Kauffman

45   Esquire

46   Think (IBM)

49   Jasper Johns. Three Flags, 1958. Encaustic on canvas. 30⅞ × 45½ × 5 in. Collection Whitney Museum of American Art. 50th Anniversary Gift of the Gilman Foundation, Inc., The Lauder Foundation, Mr. A. Alfred Taubman, an anonymous donor (and purchase). 80.32

     Jean Léon Gérôme. Pygmalion and Galatea, 1890. Oil on canvas, 35 × 27 in. © 1980 The Metropolitan Museum of Art, New York. Gift of Louis C. Raegner, 1927. 27.200

     Pygmalion, 1938. Courtesy The Museum of Modern Art Film Stills Archive

     My Fair Lady, 1964. Courtesy The Museum of Modern Art Film Stills Archive

50   Esquire. Photos Dan Wynn

51   Audience Magazine

52   Show. Photo Dan Wynn

     Signet Books

53   American Institute of Graphic Arts

54   Socotab Leaf Tobacco

     Think (IBM)

55   Maysles Brothers Films

56   Signet Books

     Show

57   Burdines

59   Zero for Conduct. Jean Vigo, 1933. Courtesy The Museum of Modern Art Film Stills Archive

     Photograph by Leombruno-Bodi. Courtesy Vogue. © 1956 (renewed 1984) The Condé Nast Publications Inc.

     Gutzon Borglum. Mount Rushmore Monument, South Dakota. Courtesy North Plains Press, Aberdeen, South Dakota

60   Fortune

61   Vanity Fair

62,63 Karastan (Ally & Gargano)

64   Vanity Fair

     Olivetti

65   Simpson Paper

66   AIGA

     Business Solutions

67   Olivetti

68   Stuart Davis. Lucky Strike, 1921. Oil on canvas, 33¼ × 18 in. Collection The Museum of Modern Art, New York. Gift of The American Tobacco Company

Numbers refer to page numbers. Unless otherwise noted, photographs were taken by the author. Where no client is mentioned photographs were personal experiments.